W9-BDO-719

THE FOCAL EASY GUIDE TO

FINAL CUT
PRO 6

THE FOCAL EASY GUIDE TO

FINAL CUT PRO 6

RICK YOUNG

ELSEVIER

AMSTERDAM • BOSTON • HEIDELBERG • LONDON • NEW YORK • OXFORD
PARIS • SAN DIEGO • SAN FRANCISCO • SINGAPORE • SYDNEY • TOKYO
Focal Press is an imprint of Elsevier

Focal Press is an imprint of Elsevier
Linacre House, Jordan Hill, Oxford OX2 8DP, UK
30 Corporate Drive, Suite 400, Burlington MA 01803, USA

First published 2008

Image on page 52 courtesy Ken Stone (www.kenstone.net)
Images on pages 227–240 taken from The Poker Show with Jesse May Copyright
Luckbox Entertainment 2005, reproduced with permission

British Library Cataloguing in Publication Data
Young, Rick, 1967–
  The Focal easy guide to Final Cut Pro 6. – (The Focal easy guide series)
  1. Final cut (Electronic resource) 2. Digital video – Editing – Data processing 3. Video
  tapes – Editing – Data processing
  I. Title II. Final Cut Pro 6
  778.5'93'0285536

Library of Congress Number: 2007937999

ISBN: 978-0-240-81009-6

For information on all Focal Press publications
visit our website at www.focalpress.com

Typeset by Charon Tec Ltd (A Macmillan Company), Chennai, India
www.charontec.com

Printed and bound in Canada
07 08 09 10 11   11 10 9 8 7 6 5 4 3 2 1

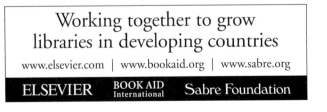

Working together to grow
libraries in developing countries

www.elsevier.com | www.bookaid.org | www.sabre.org

ELSEVIER   BOOK AID International   Sabre Foundation

Contents

Organizing your Footage   59

Editing   69

Rendering   113

Preface

It all started with a blade, in dimly lit rooms with chinagraph pencils and rickety hand-driven winders. There were no dissolves, no effects, just cuts. And masterpieces were created.

Chaplin, Eisenstein, Welles, Capra, Wilder, Hitchcock – each and every one of these great directors worked with far less sophisticated equipment than you and I, and, yet, truly great films were made.

It may have all started with a blade, yet in the modern world editing takes place on sophisticated work stations with more power than the computers used to send men to the moon! And the cost of these work stations has plummeted to an all time low. With nothing more than a DV camera, Firewire Mac and Final Cut Pro, one has tools which are infinitely superior to filmmakers of previous generations.

Yet, no matter how great the tools, it is essential to understand the principles of filmmaking. The limitations are no longer access to equipment or technology. It all comes down to skill and craftsmanship.

Go fly with this software, it's got wings....

Photo: Blanca Tamarit

When I wrote the first edition of The Easy Guide to Final Cut Pro way back when it was Final Cut Pro 2 – I had a clear vision of creating a book that was easy to follow, short on pages, and covered the essential areas of Apple's professional editing software without trying to explain every single function the software was capable of.

There were other books on the market which were so many hundreds of pages in length, that went into such detail that the beginner or professional, who simply wanted to start cutting, had the overwhelming task of having to learn to be an aircraft pilot when all they wanted to do was to take a short journey on a plane.

I wanted to side-step the detail, jump right in and get the beginner or professional up to speed using Final Cut Pro in the shortest time possible.

This book presents to the reader the essential knowledge needed to edit with Final Cut Pro. While initially aimed at those using DV as their editing format, the book is relevant to all formats and all versions of Final Cut Pro. The interface and operation of Final Cut Pro in version 6 is remarkably similar to how it was in 1999 when the very first version of the software was released. And when moving from format to format the operation of the software is virtually the same.

This is the beauty of Final Cut Pro. It is format independent and each version builds on the last. Rather than radical changes in the software, new features are added without changing the look and feel from previous versions. Final Cut Pro provides the means to cut at any level with depth and power – be it on a desktop or a laptop.

But before one can perform a single edit one needs to understand the core knowledge to make the system work. That's the challenge. Forget about the detail and focus on what is important. A builder does not examine what makes the drill spin – he or she simply squeezes the trigger and gets on with fulfilling the greater task...

So it is with Final Cut Pro – learn the essential functions and you will then be able to fulfil your creative vision whatever level you work at. To do this let's begin right at the beginning, in a time when there were no computers, no hard drives, no ram or system buses or video cameras or codecs or RAIDS or even the electronic mouse... a time when editing was new and images were all there was.

Light, chemicals and images...

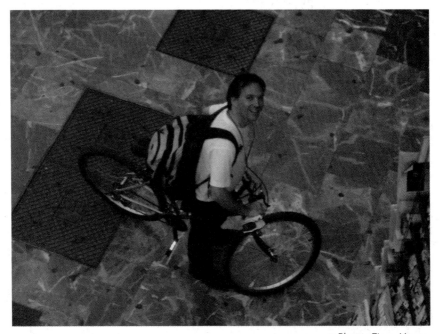

Photo: Fiona Young

Rick Young
Producer/Director/Editor
Shooting and Editing
On location, Valencia, Spain
July, 2007

GETTING
STARTED

The Digital Laboratory

Think of your computer loaded with Final Cut Pro as being like a digital laboratory. In the days when cine-film was the only means for movie-making, everyone relied on the lab. Film would be processed at the lab; there were work prints; answer prints; release prints; opticals . . . the lab was central to virtually every facet of the post-production process.

Your Mac is a digital lab, just waiting for you to stir the potions.

Essentially the post-production process is the same as it has always been. While the means to achieving results has changed, digital filmmaking requires similar methods and procedures to that of filmmaking in the world of celluloid and chemicals.

While film needed to be developed the images recorded on videotape need to be transferred from tape to hard drive – this process is known as **capture** or **transfer**.

The raw material must then be ordered and structured. In the film world this would take place in the cutting room where the editor would take reels of film and break these into smaller more manageable sections – when using Final Cut Pro an electronic equivalent to the cutting room is provided in the layout of the interface. It is here that the **editing** takes place.

Once the picture was edited the sound needed to be **mixed**. Dubbing suites with many machines running in synchronization were traditionally used. Inside your computer multiple audio tracks are electronically mixed to be output in sync with picture.

Final Cut Pro is compatible with external Sound Surfaces (using the Mackie Control Protocol, MCP). If one has an MCP compatible control surface you can ride your faders and directly mix your film inside of Final Cut Pro.

The software will record all the fader movements that you have put into the system. You can then play back your mix with full fader automation.

Effects and titles were traditionally created using a device known as an optical printer. Film exposed in the optical printer would then be immersed in developing tanks, in total darkness, to emerge, as if by magic, with hundreds of tiny transparent images. When projected these images would light up a room . . . Final Cut Pro uses electronic processes to achieve these results. Video tracks are layered in order of priority to build effects which can be made up of many different layers. This process is known as **compositing**.

Finally, the original negative would be cut and matched by technicians, wearing pure white gloves, in dust-proof rooms. Release prints were produced so the film could be distributed to cinemas and later television stations throughout the world. Release prints in the modern world are recorded onto digital tape, DVD or the final edit may need to be prepared for CD-ROM or Internet delivery. This phase of the process is known as **output**.

It should be obvious that a distinct set of processes takes place in the editing of any production. When using Final Cut Pro these processes can be broken down into five distinct areas.

(i) capture or transfer (ii) editing (iii) sound mixing (iv) compositing (v) output

Learn how to perform these essential tasks and you will be well armed with the knowledge needed to edit any program. Once these processes are learnt, you, as the editor, will be able to concentrate on the creative aspects of the editing process. Only when one moves beyond the mechanics of the editing can Final Cut Pro be used to its full potential.

Hardware and Software Requirements

At the most basic level the following hardware is needed to use Final Cut Pro:

1 A Firewire camera or deck.

2 A minimum of a G4 Mac (1.25 GHz or faster) with at least 1 GB of RAM and enough free hard drive space to store your video files. A minimum of 4 GB of disk space is required to install all the applications in the Final Cut Studio suite and a whopping additional 55 GB is required to install all optional templates, content and tutorials – these may be installed on separate disks.
Note: An AGP or PCI Express Quartz Extreme graphics card is required. For best performance use one of the Intel Macs.

3 Mac OS X 10.4.9 or later; QuickTime 7.1.6 or later; a DVD drive for installation.

Your digital video deck or camera will need DV 'in' and 'out.' Ideally you should also have a television monitor and a pair of external speakers.

If hard drive space is limited you may well choose to install Final Cut Studio without the additional content files. This could be advantageous if you are working on a Powerbook, iBook or MacBook. While it is desirable to install all the content, and therefore giving you access to the full potential of the Final Cut Studio Suite, a great deal of disk space can be saved by only installing the applications.

Inside your Mac

Your Mac is made up of many different components all specifically engineered to work together. There are hard drives, fans, a motherboard, memory, circuits, a power supply, ports and slots. Data pumps through the internal system while the keyboard and mouse act as the interface between the computer and the mind of the operator. While it is not essential to understand exactly what goes on inside your Mac it is helpful to have a general overview – particularly with regards to memory and available hard drive space. These two areas are critical to having an efficient and well-managed machine.

How Much Hard Drive Space?

The hard drives are the place where you store your video files. Any video editing system requires large hard drives capable of storing vast amounts of data. While 'the more, the better' rule applies, each and every one of us is on some sort of limit and we all have to stop somewhere.

When DV technology first became available it was all SCSI – these were hard drives with limited capacity; very expensive and a lot more difficult to set up than Firewire. These days when additional hard drives are needed it is as simple as ordering Firewire drives online or buying from your favorite computer store. One can also choose more sophisticated options such as external RAID boxes which come in several forms including SCSI, Firewire and SATA. SATA is an improved drive technology which gives sustained and reliable fast performance when using many drives RAIDED together.

5

A lot has been written over the years of the benefits of working with the operating system of your computer on one drive and storing your captured clips to a separate drive. This is really the best way to configure your system, but in the real world, a lot of people will have to use a single hard drive for the operating system and media storage for the simple reason that they only have one hard drive physically installed inside their computer. The professional MacPro towers allow for a total of four drives to be installed inside the computer – G5 towers have room for two internal drives.

Should you require more drives than your computer allows internally the simplest option is to go for external Firewire drives. Beyond this one would look toward SATA RAIDS.

Video at DV resolution chews up approximately 1 GB to 4.5 minutes of sound and video. It is easy, therefore, to work out how much material you can store on hard disk. Simply multiply the capacity of your hard drive by 4.5 and then divide the result by 60. This will calculate the amount of storage you will get in hours and minutes. The measurement of 4.5 minutes to the gigabyte is a conservative estimate. You actually get slightly more. Therefore a 60 GB drive will provide room for between 4 and 5 hours of digital video. A 200 GB drive stores approximately 15 hours at DV resolution.

If you are working with formats of higher resolution than DV then the amount of storage per gigabyte drops dramatically. While 1 minute of DV footage consumes 216 MB, 1 minute at the uncompressed standard definition will use 1.4 GB, and for top-of-the-range high definition the same 1 minute will eat up 7.3 GB of hard drive space. Furthermore, uncompressed and high definition video formats are far more demanding and often require expensive RAIDs – this is when several drives work together to provide fast and reliable transfer of large amounts of data. HDV has the same requirements as DV. Other formats such as XDCam may have variable bit rates, thus the space required will vary according to the chosen quality setting, whereas DVCPro HD, by Panasonic, uses up 4 times the space of DV.

Firewire

Firewire is an Apple invented technology which also goes under the name of iLink and IEEE1394. One of the remarkable features of Firewire technology, unlike USB, is that it is intelligent. Firewire serves not only as a data transfer bus, it also allows for device control. It is for this reason that video and audio can be transferred through a Firewire cable and deck control can take place. Furthermore, Firewire is also bi-directional which means video and audio can flow in both ways through the cable. Thus video and audio can be transferred from a deck/camera to a computer and then back again – or, alternatively, one can perform deck to deck editing.

The golden rule when connecting your Mac and camera/deck with a Firewire cable is to make sure the connector is the correct size. Without sounding too basic, make sure you insert the Firewire connector correctly – if you jam it in backwards you will end up with a bent Firewire port.

Firewire ports are identified by a symbol (which looks remarkably similar to a nuclear warning symbol).

Small and Large Firewire Connectors   **Firewire 400   Firewire 800**

Firewire cables come in several forms. Cables can be made up of any combination of small to small, large to large, or small to large connectors. The larger 6-pin Firewire port is found on the back or side of your Mac (depending which Mac you have), while the smaller 4-pin Firewire connector is located on your camera or deck. The latest version of Firewire, known as Firewire 2, or IEEE 1394b, has a maximum transfer speed of 800 Mb per second which is twice the speed of the original version, known as Firewire 400.

Simply plug the large end of the Firewire cable into your Mac and the small end into your camera or deck. Firewire cables are hot-pluggable which means they can be connected or disconnected while the Mac is switched on or off, although, ideally, the devices should be plugged together prior to launching Final Cut Pro. Otherwise a warning message will appear to alert you to the fact that no Firewire device in being seen.

Before and After Firewire

It was all analog. Everything tangled up in a mass of cables. There were wires everywhere and different standards too. We're talking 1980s' technology. Composite Video, S-Video, Component Video.

All through the 1980s the standard was Sony Betacam. First there was standard Betacam, followed by Betacam SP and eventually, well into the 1990s, Digibeta emerged as the standard for professional digital production. Sony may have lost the format war to VHS but when it came to the professional arena Sony was untouchable.

Before Betacam it was U-matic, available in low-band and hi-band versions. There were various one inch formats: A, B and C. C-format was the best by a long shot. It was like working with 35 mm film and coincidentally the tape was about the same in measurement. Before one inch there was Quad – two-inch tape that originated in the 1950s when Ampex first invented videotape.

The 1990s. Digital is everywhere. Digibeta, D1, D2, D3, D5, D9. Avid ruled the non-linear market, with Media 100 chasing at its heels. DV hadn't even been invented. Final Cut Pro wasn't even a whisper.

Everything changed in 1996 with the introduction of one camera: the Sony VX-1000. When this camera appeared on the market the world went crazy. I remember the BBC had purchased 100 of these and the camera had only just been released. Then I started hearing the BBC had a VX-1000 in every single department in the whole of the BBC. Documentaries were filmed with this camera, multi-camera shoots were produced and the professional world with all their big cameras sat back in astonishment as the world of acquisition was redefined, apparently, overnight!

DV blew the whole scene apart. The quality of DV, as a recording format, is equivalent to Beta SP. Perhaps on a technical chart DV might score slightly less, but then DV doesn't suffer from the drop-out problem which plagued Beta SP due to shedding and flaking of oxide.

DV was just the sort of technology the world wanted desperately. Finally, a low-cost, lossless, high quality camera/editing solution had arrived. This exact same technology forms the basis of Firewire editing systems today – only the deck or camera is usually connected to a computer rather than editing from camera to deck or vice versa.

When using a DV Firewire-based editing system you can work with either a camera or deck – providing the deck/camera has both Firewire 'in' and 'out.' The advantages of having a deck are (i) you don't beat up your camera every time you capture footage (ii) a deck offers other features such as different inputs, the ability to work with large or small size tapes, a large time-code display, a jog/shuttle wheel and often a built-in edit controller. More recent formats use solid-state media and therefore have no moving parts.

Video Formats

The world we live in operates with several different video formats.

DV-NTSC applies to the USA, Japan and many other parts of the world; whereas DV-PAL is used throughout most of Europe, Australia, and parts of Asia. There are other formats such as SECAM which is used in France, Russia and North Africa, and variations on PAL and NTSC are used in South America. However, PAL and NTSC remain the dominant formats.

If you are working with HDV the standard for the USA and the rest of the 'NTSC world' is 60i. If you are working with HDV in the 'PAL world' the standard is 50i.

Final Cut Pro is geared to edit everything from DV to standard and high definition video. It is also capable of film production.

Television Aspect Ratio

Another consideration is whether the footage you are working with has been filmed in widescreen anamorphic – 16:9, or standard television format – 4:3. Do not confuse letterbox (cropped 4:3) with true widescreen. Many consumer cameras do not offer a true widescreen anamorphic mode of operation. However, many offer a cropped 4:3 letterbox setting.

| Standard 4:3 Television Format | Widescreen Anamorphic | Cropped 4:3 or Letterbox |

Note: All the HD formats are widescreen.

Loading the Software

1 Put the Final Cut Studio Install DVD into the DVD drive of your Mac.

Install Final Cut Studio

2 Double click the Install Final Cut Studio icon.

Follow the on-screen instruction making sure you agree to the licence agreement.

3 Highlight the hard drive where you wish to install the software and click continue.

Macintosh HD
148GB (31.3GB Free)

Continue

4 Choose the option No when asked if you want to make your computer available for distributed processing over a network, unless you specifically wish to be able to do this.

You now need to decide which of the associated media you wish to install. All of the applications will be installed, meaning Final Cut Pro, DVD Studio Pro, Compressor, Motion, Soundtrack Pro, Color, Livetype,

Cinema Tools and Apple Qmaster – however, it is up to you to decide if you want all of the media for each of the applications to be installed. Remember, installing everything will take more hard drive space. If you have plenty of space this isn't an issue.

To choose specific content you wish to install click the arrows to the left of each of the applications and then check or uncheck accordingly.

5 You will then be prompted to insert the different DVDs according to which options you checked for installation.

The software you are installing requires additional installation discs. Please have these discs ready:

Audio Content 1
Audio Content 2
Audio Content 3
LiveType Media 1
LiveType Media 2
Motion Content

(Cancel)   (Continue Installation)

Simply follow the instructions as they appear. If you are installing all of the content for the Final Cut Studio suite it will take a considerable amount of time for the entire installation process to complete. You need to feed the appropriate DVDs into your Mac in the order requested.

6 Finally, you will be prompted to choose the format you will be working with by clicking on the drop-down menu which appears.

This can be easily changed once you start using the software.

7 Click OK.

Initial Setup

Once Final Cut Pro has been successfully installed you need to be able to access Final Cut Pro and the other applications which are installed on your system.

Final Cut Pro and all of the other applications you have installed can be accessed by going to the application folder which is located on the hard drive where the operating system of your computer is installed.

The easiest way to get to the Applications folder is to choose the menu at the top of the desktop screen titled Go.

1　Select the Go menu and scroll down to Applications.

2　Locate the Final Cut Pro application icon in the Applications folder.

3　Drag the Final Cut Pro icon onto the dock.

4　Do the same with the other applications you have installed, such as Livetype, Soundtrack Pro, DVD Studio Pro, Compressor and Color.

5　Click once on the Final Cut Pro icon to launch the program. You are now ready to begin work within Final Cut Pro.

Easy Setup

Apple have made it very easy to set up Final Cut Pro, however, it is up to you to make sure you get these settings right. If you set the audio sample rate incorrectly the result will be sync drift; if you set the video to widescreen anamorphic when it was shot in standard 4:3 your images will not fit the frame correctly.

The simplest way to set up Final Cut Pro is to access the Easy Setup menu.

Open the Final Cut Pro menu at the top left of the screen. Scroll to Easy Setup and release your mouse button.

Take a good look at the options presented to you in the Easy Setup menu.

There are three areas which need to be investigated:

Final Cut Pro	File	Edit	View

About Final Cut Pro

User Preferences...   ⌥Q
System Settings...   ⇧Q

Easy Setup...   ⌃Q
Audio/Video Settings...   ⌥⌘Q

Provide Feedback

Services   ▶

Hide Final Cut Pro   ⌘H
Hide Others   ⌥⌘H
Show All

Quit Final Cut Pro   ⌘Q

Easy Setup

Format: (all formats) ▼   Rate: (all rates) ▼

Use: DV-PAL Anamorphic ▼

Use this Easy Setup when working with Anamorphic DV PAL source material with audio set to 48 kHz using FireWire for input/output of audio and video and Device Control set to FireWire.

Format: refers to the standard of video you are working with. You may work in HD, PAL or NTSC or a specific variation which can be defined.

Rate: there are four possible frame rates. By defining the rate you tell Final Cut Pro the amount of frames per second which the video will run at.

Use: within a particular format there can be many possible uses. This option lets you define specifically how the chosen format will be used.

By clicking each of these options you will see that a drop down menu will appear displaying the options for each of these categories present. It is important to be aware that the options presented in the **Use** menu will be determined by the selection you have have made with the first two options: **Format** and **Rate.**

DV-PAL
DV-PAL Anamorphic
DV-PAL FireWire Basic
DV50 - PAL
DV50 PAL Anamorphic
DVCPRO - PAL
DVCPRO - PAL (No Device)
DVCPRO - PAL 48 kHz Anamorphic
DVCPRO HD - 1080i50
DVCPRO HD - 720p25
HDV – 1080i50
HDV – 1080i50 FireWire Basic
HDV – 1080p25
HDV – 720p25
HDV-Apple Intermediate Codec 1080i50
IMX PAL (30 Mb/s)
IMX PAL (40 Mb/s)
IMX PAL (50 Mb/s)
OfflineRT - DVCPRO - PAL
OfflineRT HD – 25
OfflineRT PAL
OfflineRT PAL Anamorphic
Uncompressed 10–bit PAL 48 kHz
Uncompressed 8–bit PAL 48 kHz
XDCAM HD 1080i50 CBR
XDCAM HD 1080i50 VBR
XDCAM HD 1080p25 CBR
XDCAM HD 1080p25 VBR

(all formats)
HD
NTSC
PAL
OfflineRT

Apple Intermediate Codec
DV/Panasonic DVCPRO
HDV
MPEG IMX
Panasonic DVCPRO HD
Panasonic DVCPRO-50
Photo - JPEG
Sony XDCAM HD
Uncompressed 10–bit 4:2:2
Uncompressed 8–bit 4:2:2

(all rates)
23.98 fps
24.00 fps
25.00 fps

What Apple has done is to provide choice to the user and in providing choices this forces the user to make a decision. The images above and left show all the possible choices. Straight away one can see that there are several frame-rates, many different formats and the use provided by the formats is extensive.

Now look what happens when one chooses a specific frame-rate or format to work with – the Use then becomes narrower. When choosing HD as the **Format** at the **Rate** of 25 frames per second then the only options which will be offered

DVCPRO HD – 1080i50
DVCPRO HD – 720p25
HDV – 1080i50
HDV – 1080i50 FireWire Basic
HDV – 1080p25
HDV – 720p25
HDV-Apple Intermediate Codec 1080i50
XDCAM HD 1080i50 CBR
XDCAM HD 1080i50 VBR
XDCAM HD 1080p25 CBR
XDCAM HD 1080p25 VBR

in the **Use** column are those which correspond to this format and frame-rate.

Again, in another example, when choosing to work in NTSC at the frame rate of 29.97 the following options are offered:

With previous versions of Final Cut Pro all the options for Easy Setup were offered in one long list. Because there are now many more video frame-rates and formats than in the past, the Easy Setup procedure has been streamlined to categorize the choices. The three headings: **Format**, **Rate** and **Use** means that the user has to simply select the **Format** they are working with, choose the **Frame-Rate** and then select from the **Use** column that which corresponds to their requirments.

Once that is done simply press the Setup button and you are done.

Do not be confused or intimidated by the many formats, multiple frame-rates and wide selection of uses on offer. You are simply telling Final Cut Pro the standard you wish to edit at. Once done you can then move forward with the editing process.

Note: when you make the first edit to the Timeline of a new Sequence, if the frame-rate or format does not match the Sequence setting, you will then be offered the choice to change the Sequence Setting regardless of what you set the Easy Setup to. Effectively this provides a quick and easy way of changing the settings without going through the Easy Setup process. However, it is extremely useful to use the Easy Setup as you can then specifically determine the Sequence setting manually

Warning – This clip does not match this sequence's settings.

For best performance your sequence and External Video should be set to the format of the clips you are editing.

Change sequence settings to match the clip settings?

No   Yes

so this matches the format you wish to work at. It could be a disadvantage to have Final Cut Pro make this choice for you.

DV Audio

It is important to understand how DV audio works. Otherwise you can end up in a lot of trouble when you begin the capture process. DV audio can be recorded at two different sample rates:

16 bit – 48 kHz provides the highest quality and allows for two channels of audio, or a single stereo pair to be recorded.
12 bit – 32 kHz provides lesser quality, though still very good, and allows for two sets of stereo pairs, or four individual tracks to be recorded.

By default, the DV-PAL and DV-NTSC Easy Setups are set to the highest possible sample rate of 48 kHz.

For the most, 16 bit audio is the preferred option, unless one specifically needs to access four independent channels. While this may sound ideal it is rare for any DV cameras to actually have inputs to record four independent channels of audio. The main advantage to setting a camera to 12 bit – 32 kHz is that audio dubbing can then take place onto the remaining free set of stereo pairs.

Unless you specifically plan on accessing these tracks I recommend setting your camera to 16 bit – 48 kHz. This is usually accessed through the menu settings in your camera.

The Audio Sample Rate is Set in the Menu of your DV Camera

THE INTERFACE

I fell in love with Final Cut Pro the first time I saw it and knew that it was going to be an app. that changed the world.
GARY ADCOCK
CHICAGO FINAL CUT PRO USER GROUP

As much of the post-production industry moved from film to video production a new way of working came into being. Moviolas and flat-beds had competition to deal with as a new kid appeared on the block. The kid was called the two-machine video editing suite.

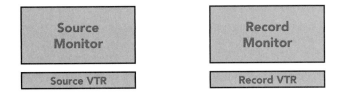

In this environment the editor would line up a shot on a source machine and edit across to a record machine. 'In' and 'out' points were marked, tapes pre-rolled, then run up to speed and images in the form of electronic signals were copied from one machine to the other.

The Final Cut Pro interface is modelled on the same idea.

The Interface is Made up of Four Main Windows

Notice the two windows located at the top right of the Final Cut Pro interface. Think of the window on the left, the Viewer, as being the source monitor and the window on the right, the Canvas, as being the record monitor. In essence, a shot is lined up in the Viewer and copied across to the Canvas. The area immediately below the Viewer and Canvas is known as the Timeline. This shows the edited shots as blocks in the order in which they have been edited. The left window above the Timeline is called the Browser. Think of this as being like a cabinet which stores the masses of footage ready for the editor to access.

Also, take note of the Audio Meters and Tool Palette.

All professional VTRs have meters which must be watched to make sure the audio doesn't distort during the transfer and playback of sound and picture. The golden rule is always to make sure the audio meters do not peak into the red (DV audio should peak at -12 dB).

To swing the analogy back to the film days the Tool Palette represents the tools the editor would physically work with: the splicer, the hand-winders, the spools and frame measuring instruments. The Tool Palette in Final Cut Pro gives the editor access to the instruments with which the finer details of the editing process are crafted. It should be clear by now that Final Cut Pro draws on the very best the world of post-production has offered in the history of film and video production.

If you find the terms Browser, Viewer, Canvas, and Timeline difficult to identify with, just think of the Browser as the place where all clips are stored, the Viewer is where one watches the individual video clips, the Canvas is where the material is edited and the Timeline is the place where the individual shots which make up the entire movie are arranged.

Arranging the Interface

The Final Cut Pro interface can be set up in several different ways. Individual users can work according to their own particular preference. Several different arrangements can be chosen from within Final Cut Pro or the editor can create their own custom layouts.

1 Go to the Window menu (located top right) and scroll down to Arrange. You will notice there is a list of options for arranging the interface.

2 Scroll to any of these options and release your mouse button. Each time you wish to try a different layout you need to return to the Window menu, scroll to Arrange and then move across to the layout you wish to select.

My preference is to use the Standard setting, however, I do modify this setup slightly.

I position the Toolbar to the left, the Timeline in the center and the Audio Meters to the right. This produces a neat, symmetrical display.

To achieve this setup is simple:

1 Drag the Toolbar by clicking in the gray area at the top and position it on the opposite side of the screen beneath the Browser and next to the Timeline.

2 Slide the Timeline to the right so that it is positioned directly between the Toolbar and the Audio Meters.

3 If necessary resize the Timeline window by dragging the bottom right corner so there is no overlap onto either the Toolbar or Audio Meters.

Once you have set the layout according to your personal preference it is then possible to save the setup as a Custom Layout.

Learning a Custom Layout

To set a Custom Layout, so that it can be recalled at any time, is easy to achieve. Press the key/mouse combination in the following order:

1 Hold down the Alt/Option key (located to the left of the Space Bar).

2 While still holding down the Alt/Option key, select the Window menu at the top of the screen.

3 Scroll to Arrange. Where it normally displays Custom Layout 1 it will now read Set Custom Layout 1. Point your cursor to this setting and release the mouse button. Your Custom Layout will now be set.

You can confirm this has been achieved by selecting any of the other layouts. Now go back to the Window menu, scroll to Arrange and select Custom Layout 1. Your screen should revert back to the Custom Layout you have just set. If it does not, backtrack using the instructions above and try again. Once your Custom Layout has been set it will be remembered each time you open up Final Cut Pro and you can then choose your Custom Layout, or any of the setups which are listed under the Arrange options.

It is possible to set up to two Custom Layouts, for easy access, or to save to hard drive an infinite amount of setups. This can be convenient when there is more than one editor who uses the same system or if you find different layouts suitable for different aspects of working within the program.

To save a Window Layout you need to:

1 Set up the layout according to your needs on-screen.

2 Select the Window menu.

3 Scroll to Arrange.

Save Window Layout...
Load Window Layout...

4 Choose Save Window Layout.

5 To recall a Window Layout choose Load Window Layout.

Save Window Layout...
Load Window Layout...

6 Navigate to the setup of your choice.

7 Click Choose.

Important Details about the Interface

It is worth having a good understanding of the interface of Final Cut Pro. This gives you the power to use Final Cut Pro to its full potential and to achieve a variety of editing tasks in many different ways.

Look to the extreme left of the Timeline – notice there are green radio buttons next to each of the tracks. These are monitoring buttons for video and audio. If you press the green button on any of the tracks you are effectively switching it off – this will deactivate the monitoring for that particular track and gives you the ability to mute the audio, or kill the video, at the flick of a switch.

At the base of the Timeline is a little speaker icon. Click this and you will see a selection of controls open in the Timeline next to the green monitoring buttons. These controls give you the means to quickly isolate an audio track for monitoring purposes. The speaker icon does the same as the green radio buttons, whereas by clicking the headphone indicator this will switch off all tracks except that which you have just selected. This can be more efficient than isolating each of the tracks individually.

At the bottom left of the Timeline there is a symbol that looks like two mountains – this is called Clip Overlays. Later, as you get into the editing and sound mixing process, you will find this facility extremely useful for adjusting audio levels and setting the opacity of video clips.

To the right of Clip Overlays are four little boxes. These boxes affect the size of the clips as they are displayed in the Timeline. This is useful for increasing the visual size of the clips if you are working with a monitor which is cramped for screen real estate.

The following point is very important to take note of: look to the top of the Viewer and Canvas, just below the tabbed sections. You will notice there is a button with a percentage value in it. Click this button and it will reveal a series of numeric values – always keep this set to Fit To Window and have Show As

Square Pixels checked at the bottom. If you do not select Fit To Window you may encounter jerky playback and experience a great deal of frustration working out the solution. This applies to both the Viewer and the Canvas.

Considering that we have not even begun the editing process, the relevance of these details may seem a bit obscure at this stage. Rest assured it will make sense as you become familiar with the inner workings of Final Cut Pro.

Button Bars

To speed up your workflow it is possible to add buttons to the top of the main windows of the interface. This enables you to quickly access functions which are often used.

1 Select the Tools menu and scroll to Button List. A list of assignable functions will appear.

2 Click any of the arrows to the left of each of the headings to reveal a list of the mappable functions.

3 Choose a function you wish to move to a button bar.

4 Drag the item from the Button List to the bar at the top of one of the windows of the interface. The button will then slot into place.

5 Press the button to perform the function assigned to it.

Customizing the Keyboard Layout

For editors migrating from other editing systems, this feature can make the learning curve with Final Cut Pro a much smoother transition. Every single button on the keyboard can be remapped to perform specific functions.

1 Select the Tools menu and scroll to Keyboard Layout.

2 Move right and choose Customize.

3 Click on the lock to unlock the keyboard.

Click any of the arrows next to the menu list to reveal a list of assignable functions.

4 Choose a function and drag it to a key of your choice.

5 Close the keyboard layout by clicking top left. The changes will then saved.

If you happen to change the settings and wish to revert back to the defaults then press Reset.

Note: Both settings, the button bars and the ability to customize the keyboard layout can also be accessed by Control clicking in the gray area next to each of the bars at the top of the windows.

Remove ▶

Show Keyboard Layout

Show Button List

Save Main Button Bars...
Load Main Button Bars...

Saving Projects and Accessing the Autosave Vault

OS X is regarded as being extremely stable and reliable. However, just like any computer, there are times when an application may freeze or crash. This doesn't happen often with Final Cut Pro (in fact I regularly edit for days and weeks without the slightest hitch), however, in the event of something going wrong you need to be able retrieve the most up-to-date version of your project.

File Edit View

New
New Project
Open...
Open Recent
Close Window
Close Tab
Close Project

Save Project

The saying 'save early, save often' is a motto to live by. As soon as you begin work on a project save it. Get in the habit of regularly pressing Apple + S or selecting Save Project from the File menu.

Final Cut Pro File Edit View

About Final Cut Pro

User Preferences... ⌥Q

☑ Autosave Vault
Save a copy every: | 5 | minutes
Keep at most: | 100 | copies per project
Maximum of: | 100 | projects

Beyond this it is advisable to switch on the Autosave Vault option found under User Preferences (accessed under the Final Cut Pro menu). This will automatically save a copy of your project at the intervals you specify. I set this to save every 5 minutes and to keep 100 copies of my project. My philosophy is one can't be too careful!

In the event of a catastrophe simply open up your project, go to the File menu and choose Restore Project. A list will appear of all the Autosaved versions of your project with the most recent version being displayed at the top of the list. Click to open the version of your choice, then click OK and you will then be back on track. Having the Autosave function could save you a great deal of heartache.

File	Edit	View	Mark	M
New			▶	
New Project			⇧⌘N	
Open...			⌘O	
Open Recent			▶	
Close Window			Today, 12:47	
Close Tab			Today, 12:37	
Close Project			Today, 12:27	
			Today, 12:27	
Save Project			Today, 11:35	
Save Project As...			Yesterday, 14:45	
Save All			Yesterday, 14:33	
Revert Project			Yesterday, 14:23	
Restore Project...			Yesterday, 14:18	
			Yesterday, 01:02	
			Yesterday, 00:57	

Note: for reference, the Autosave Vault is buried away in your Final Cut Pro documents folder. The method described is the easiest way to access it.

Why its meteoric rise? It worked right out of the box.
MICHAEL HORTON
LOS ANGELES FINAL CUT PRO USER GROUP

Nothing can be done with any editing program if you do not have the video material stored on the hard drives of your computer. It is therefore essential to capture the material before you can begin the editing process. Before you can begin capturing you must instruct the computer where the captured video files will be stored – in Final Cut Pro this area is called the Scratch Disks.

Setting Scratch Disks

Setting Scratch disks is simple and straightforward. Getting this right is the key to successful media management. You need to know where your files are stored.

File	Edit	View	Mark	Mo(
New	▶
New Project	⇧⌘N
Open...	⌘O
Open Recent	▶
Close Window	⌘W
Close Tab	^W
Close Project	
Save Project	⌘S
Save Project As...	⇧⌘S
Save All	⌥⌘S
Revert Project	
Restore Project...	
Import	▶
Export	▶
Send To	▶
Batch Export	
Batch Capture...	^C
Log and Capture...	⌘8
Log and Transfer...	⇧⌘8
Media Manager...	

1 Go to the File menu which is found at the top left of the screen.

2 Scroll down to Log and Capture and release your mouse button. The Log and Capture window will now open.

Time (AV) 59.5 min

00:00:00:00

Logging | Clip Settings | Capture Settings

Log Bin: FCPFiles

Reel: 001

Name:

Description:

Scene:

3 Click on the Capture Settings tab which is located to the right of the Log and Capture window.

4 Click the Scratch Disks button. This will reveal the Scratch Disks window.

Scratch Disks...

5 Press the Set button closest to the top – the reason there are several Set buttons is to allow one to set multiple scratch disks.

6 Navigate to the hard drives on your computer.

7 Double click a hard drive. This will set the hard drive as the first scratch disk in the list. If possible, select a drive that does not contain the operating system for your Mac (this ensures optimum performance when editing).

iDisk

Network

Macintosh HD

SF

What you have done is to tell Final Cut Pro where to store your video files. You have selected a hard drive to store your footage. Final Cut Pro will then automatically create three folders on this drive:

Capture Scratch – the video files you use to edit.
Audio Render – for audio render files.
Render – for video which is processed during rendering.

When you start a new Final Cut Pro project, once that project is saved and you have commenced the capture process, a folder will then appear inside of the

Capture Scratch folder on the hard drive you selected. That folder is named the same as the project you are working on. Thus, all the files you Capture (or Transfer) end up inside the Capture Scratch folder in another folder named the same as your project. Similarly as you render material – for video or audio – then a folder is created in each of the Audio Render and Video Render folders, on the hard drive you have designated to be the Scratch disk. These are also named the same as your project.

- ▶ 🗀 Applications
- ▶ 🗀 Audio Render Files
- ▼ 🗀 Capture Scratch
  - ▶ 🗀 Cinekinetic
  - ▶ 🗀 CorporatePromo
  - ▶ 🗀 Filming in Valencia
  - ▶ 🗀 PitchDubs
  - ▶ 🗀 Rick'sReaction

- 🗀 Applications ▷
- 🗀 Audio Render Files ▶
- 🗀 Capture Scratch ▷
- 🗀 Cinesaddle3Films ▷
- 🗀 Desktop Folder ▷
- 🗀 EllenMedia ▷
- ▦ Garvin 1
- ▦ Garvin 2
- ▦ Garvin 3
- 🗎 Installer Log File
- 🗀 iPhotoBackupFeb1507 ▷
- 🗀 LauraDVDFiles ▷
- 🗀 Library ▷
- 🗀 Render Files ▷

- 🗀 Cinekinetic
- 🗀 CorporatePromo
- 🗀 Filming in Valencia
- 🗀 PitchDubs
- 🗀 Rick'sReaction

So as you work on multiple projects you will end up with folders based on your project name inside of the three folders – **Capture Scratch, Audio Render** and **Render**. Effectively what happens is Final Cut Pro, in an eloquent fashion, takes care of the difficulties of Media Management by always filing items away in the these three folders named the same as your project.

You can nominate up to 12 separate Scratch disks, the benefit of having multiple Scratch Disks is as one drive fills up then automatically Final Cut Pro will move onto the next available Scratch Disk to store further material.

The major difficulty people get into with Scratch Disks is when multiple projects are open at a time. It is possible to capture files into a project, other than the one you are working on. These files will then be mixed in with the files of another project.

There are two ways to avoid this:

(1) Only work with a single project open at a time thus ensuring your files will only be captured or transferred into that project.

(2) Create and select a Logging Bin to capture into. This is done by this control-clicking on a bin and selecting Set Logging Bin.

Make Offline...
Set Logging Bin
Batch Export

Finally, if one wishes, Scratch Discs can be set manually. This is achieved by following the method described earlier in steps 1–7 – however, when you get to the final stage where you double click the hard drive to set it as the

New Folder

Scratch Disc – you need to click the New Folder button – name it, and then the three folders for Audio Render, Capture Scratch and Render will appear inside the folder and location you have defined.

Setting scratch disks will become second nature once you have run through the process a few times. The methods described gives you the power to define exactly where you want your files to be stored. Providing you are disciplined you will be able to manage the media for each project you work on.

Working with Formats other than DV

Final Cut Pro 6 has been designed to natively capture material which originates on many different formats including DV, DVCam, HDV, DVCPro 50, DVCPro HD, XDCam, XDCam HD and MPG IMX.

When working with formats which do not work over Firewire or which require another protocol to capture into Final Cut Pro, you have two options. You can transfer the original material to an intermediary format such as DV/DVCam or DVCPro HD for editing, or you can purchase additional hardware which will enable you to capture the footage.

The choice is up to you which option you wish to pursue. Working at the higher levels of uncompressed standard or high definition may be quite alluring, however, be aware that the requirements to edit these formats may go beyond simply installing a card or external device to your Mac. There can be certain hard drive requirements and configuration issues when working outside the realms of DV and Firewire. This can bump up the cost of setting up a system considerably.

These points considered, Final Cut Pro provides a competitive and cost-effective solution for working with multiple standards of video or film. It is up to you whether you wish to move away from the simplicity of capturing and editing over Firewire.

Getting the Most Out of the Capture Process

An important part of preparing for the editing process is to watch your material. To edit your footage properly you have to know what there is to work with. I always use the capture stage as a dual purpose procedure: (1) to watch the footage, properly, in real time as it is captured and (2) to capture the footage onto hard drive.

In the film world, as soon as the footage made it back from the lab, the dailies would then be screened. A projector was laced up and the illuminated images thrown forth in a display of light onto the screen. Based on what the director saw the rest of the shooting could then be arranged.

You are the director, the Log and Capture facility is your projector. So watch your images and build the structure of your film in your mind before you cut a single shot to another shot. You decide what to take in, what to leave out, and what to reshoot if necessary.

Methods of Capturing Footage from Tape

There are three ways to capture DV or any tape-based footage when using Final Cut Pro: **Capture Clip, Capture Now** and **Batch Capture**.

Capture Clip, as the name suggests, is used to capture a single clip at a time. It requires the editor to first mark 'in' and 'out' points. An 'in' point refers to the position on the tape where the capture process is to begin and the 'out' point is where the capture process is to stop. Once the 'in' and 'out' points are marked the computer cues up the tape in the deck/camera to the appropriate point and transfers the material onto hard drive.

Capture Now is used to capture clips 'on-the-fly'. This means the capture process begins the moment the editor instructs the computer to begin capturing and stops when the Escape button is pressed.

Batch Capture is used to capture multiple clips. Each clip is first 'logged' and the computer is then instructed to capture each of the clips in succession.

Deck Control

To capture video files to hard drive it is essential to know how to control the replay deck or camera from the computer. This is quite simple and has been well integrated into the editing interface. All operations are easily accessible using keyboard commands.

Space Bar	**Play**
J	**Play Backwards**
K	**Stop**
L	**Play Forwards**
i	**Mark 'in' point**
o	**Mark 'out' point**

Each of the play commands J and L work in increments. By pressing J or L up to five times will speed up the result. This will be obvious as we get further into the Final Cut Pro workflow.

The Capture Window

The Capture window is the facility provided within Final Cut Pro to enable you perform the capture process. It is important to understand the controls within this window and how to use them.

1   To open the Capture window first make sure your deck/camera is switched on. If you are using a camera make sure it is in VTR mode.

2   Choose the File menu at the top left of the screen. Scroll to Log and Capture.

Log and Capture.

The Capture window will now open.

Above is marked the crucial areas one needs to understand to effectively use the Log and Capture window.

Clip Duration – when logging clips for Batch Capture or using Capture Clip, 'in' and 'out' points must first be marked. The duration of the clip is calculated by Final Cut Pro and displayed in the Clip Duration window.

Time Code Display – whenever a DV tape is playing, a running display will show the timecode numbers ticking over. If you stop the tape the timecode at the exact point where the tape is parked will be displayed.

'In' Point – an 'in' point is marked by pressing the letter 'i'. The marked 'in' point is displayed in this window.

'Out' Point – an 'out' point is marked by pressing the letter 'o'. The marked 'out' point is displayed in this window.

Virtual VTR Controller – just like most VTRs have stop, play and shuttle commands – this virtual controller performs similar functions.

Capture Clip/Capture Now/Batch Capture – used to perform the capture functions.

Also note the display at the top of the Capture window which tells you how much free space is available on your computer and how much this capacity equals in minutes. The amount of space is the sum total available on the scratch disk or disks you set earlier.

You can therefore determine whether you have room on your hard drives to capture the material required for your project.

Total Free Space	126.6 GB		Total Free Time	(AV) 585.9 min
00:00:00:00				00:00:11:

Capture Clip

If you wish to capture a single clip at a time this is easily achieved using the Capture Clip method. When using this method you need to first mark the 'in' and 'out' points for the clip you wish to capture.

1. Put a tape into your deck or camera and make sure it is switched on. If you are using a camera make sure it is in VTR mode.

2. Open the Capture window which is accessed through the File menu. Alternatively, press the Apple key and the number 8 and this will achieve the same result (the Apple key is located immediately left of the Space Bar).

3. Press the Space Bar and your deck or camera will spring to life. If it doesn't, press play on your deck/camera to engage the heads. From this point on remote control of your Firewire device will work direct from the keyboard.

Once the tape is playing at speed, the result of having pressed the Space Bar, you can then spool through the tape using the J K L method. As mentioned earlier, pressing the letter J will run the tape backwards, K is for stop (or use the Space Bar to start/stop the tape) and the letter L is to run the tape forwards. By pressing the letters J and L multiple times affects the replay speed incrementally. If you press the letter J once the tape will spool backwards at normal speed, press it again and the tape will continue backwards, however, slightly faster. Press it again and the speed will increase until the maximum speed is attained after five taps. Likewise, when using the letter L the tape will shuttle forward in increments until a maximum speed is achieved after five taps.

4   When you get to the point where you want the capture to begin press the letter 'i' – this will mark the 'in' point. Similarly, press the letter 'o' to mark the 'out' point. If you look to the bottom of the Capture window, the timecode reference for the marked 'in' and 'out' points will be displayed.

Note: when marking 'in' and 'out' points you can mark the points on-the-fly. This means you can mark 'in' and 'out' points by pressing the letters 'i' and 'o' at the appropriate points while the tape is running. If you prefer, while the tape is playing, hold down the letter 'i' and release it when you get to the point where you wish the 'in' point to be marked. The same applies for the 'out' point. Hold down the letter 'o' and release it to mark the 'out' point. Final Cut Pro is flexible in that the same result can be achieved in a variety of ways.

5   Once the 'in' and 'out' points have been marked press the Clip button at the bottom of the Capture Window. You will then be prompted to name the clip.

6   Name the clip and press OK. The Mac will then instruct the deck/camera to cue up the clip which will then be captured to disk and placed into the Browser for you to access.

By repeating this process you can capture as many clips as you wish.

Capture Now

An alternative way to capture clips is to use the Capture Now facility. This is a simple method that does not require you first to mark the 'in' and 'out' points.

1   Open the Capture window and play the tape in your deck/camera.

2   Press the Now button which sits immediately to the
right of the Clip button in the Capture window.
Immediately upon pressing 'Now' the capture process will begin.
The images on the DV tape will be mirrored in a large window on your
computer monitor. A message at the bottom of this window will
confirm that capture is taking place.

> **Capturing Clip – NOW CAPTURING (press 'esc' to stop)**
> **WARNING: Capture Now is limited to 30 min**

3   Once the material you want has
played, press the Escape key (located
top left of your keyboard) to exit
Capture Now. The capture process
will stop and the clip will be placed into
the Browser.

You can then name the clip by overtyping the
name assigned to it by Final Cut Pro.

Always remember to close the Capture window once you have completed the
capture process (do this by clicking the extreme top left of the Capture
window). Failure to do so will prevent video and audio from playing through
the Firewire – to your deck or camera – and onto your television monitor
(assuming you are working with this configuration). By closing the Capture
window this problem will be avoided.

Batch Capture

Batch Capture is an extremely useful facility for capturing many clips at a time.
It is necessary to first log the clips you wish to capture, name them and then
invoke the Batch Capture function.

1 Cue the tape in your deck/camera to the point where you wish to mark the first 'in' point. Mark the 'in' point and 'out' point for the first clip you wish to capture.

2 Press the Log Clip button – located at the bottom of the Log and Capture window.

3 You will now be prompted to give the clip a name. Do this and notice the clip appears with the name you assigned to it in the Browser window with a diagonal red line through it. The red line indicates that the clip is logged but not yet captured to disk.

4 Log as many clips as you wish to capture from the tape in your camera/deck.

5 Once you have logged the clips you wish to capture stop your DV tape by pressing the Space Bar or stop button on your deck/camera.

6 Look at the Browser area where your clips are logged – each clip will have a diagonal red line through it. Notice that the last clip you logged is highlighted. Click once anywhere in the Browser to deselect it. This is particularly important – otherwise when you try to Batch Capture, only the highlighted clip(s) will be captured.

7 In the Log and Capture window press the Batch button located bottom right. You will now be prompted with a screen full of information. Check

that the Capture Preset corresponds with the format you are working with. If not, click the Capture Preset bar to select the format you are working with. Click OK to continue.

8 A window will now appear stating the number of clips which are ready to capture. Press the Continue button.

9 After a short pause your deck/camera will cue up the first of your clips and the Batch process will commence. As each clip is captured the device will stop and shuttle to the next clip and so forth until all the clips have been captured.

10 Once all the clips have been captured you will be prompted with a dialog box which tells you the numbers of clips that have been successfully captured. Click the finished button and, as if by magic, all the red lines will disappear from the clips in the Browser, signifying that they are stored on hard disk and accessible to work with.

If working with DV, always remember to close the Capture window once you have completed the capture process or video and audio will not play through the Firewire cable to your deck or camera.

Selectively Capturing using Batch Capture

When you are working with Batch Capture you can be selective about what items you wish to capture. You can choose to capture Selected Items, Offline Items or All Items in the Logging Bin.

1 Highlight the items in the Browser which you wish to capture by holding down the Apple key and clicking on the individual clips.

2 Open the Log and Capture window.

3 Click the Capture bar at the top of the Capture window and choose Selected Items in Logging Bin.

4 Press OK followed by Continue.

Setting a Logging Bin

It can be advantageous to specify a Bin where material will be placed into directly on capture. This works for Capture Clip, Capture Now and Batch Capture.

Working with Bins is dealt with in the next chapter. For now it is sufficient to say that Bins in Final Cut Pro are the equivalent of folders as used throughout the Mac operating system. Bins provide a place to file things away.

Capturing into a Logging Bin is particularly important when working with Batch Capture as there are times when Final Cut Pro will try to capture items in the Browser, including material which has already been captured. This could be due to the user failing to number reels correctly or trying to Capture Clips with matching timecode to clips which have already been captured.

To create a Logging Bin:

1 Click in the Browser to make it active.

2 Select the File menu and scroll to New Bin. You will see the Bin appear in the Browser window.

3 Name the Bin by clicking and overtyping.

4 Control click on the Bin and choose Set Logging Bin from the menu which appears.

The Logging Bin is now set and this is made obvious by the little Final Cut Pro clapperboard which sits to the left of the clip.

Use the Log and Capture window to Log the clip(s) you wish to capture. Notice they go directly into the Bin you have designated as the Logging Bin. All logged clips will go directly into this Bin.

5 Log your clips directly into the Logging Bin.

6 Press Batch and all of your clips will then be captured into the Logging Bin.

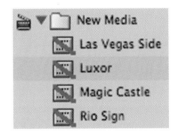

By following the above instructions will give you trouble-free capture at all times. This is the method I recommend when using Batch Capture.

To create a new Logging Bin create a new Bin and repeat the above procedure.

Clearing a Logging Bin

It is very simple to clear the Logging Bin so that clips will be captured directly into the Browser.

1   Click the Logging tab in the Log and Capture window.

2   Press the button to the immediate right of the area which displays the Logging Bin name.

This will reset the Logging Bin so that the little Final Cut Pro clapperboard is placed at the top of the Browser. This is the default position and only changes when a Logging Bin has been set.

Logging Bin Set   Logging Reset

The Clip Settings Tab

The middle tab in the Log and Capture window provides controls which let you be specific about how your material is captured. You can choose to capture audio or video only and you can also choose whether you want your audio to be captured as Stereo Pairs or separate Mono Channels.

Click the button labelled **Preview** and this allows you to hear your audio direct through the Mac on both playback and capture. This is advantageous if you do not have a set of external speakers plugged into you deck or camera.

Stereo Pairs

Split Mono

Capturing Multi-channels of Audio

A big criticism of previous versions of Final Cut Pro was the fact that it could only capture 2 channels of audio at a time. For formats such as Digibeta, which records 4 channels of audio, this was a serious limitation. To capture more than 2 channels at a time would require several passes.

Providing you are using Final Cut Pro version 5 or 6, one can now capture up to 24 channels of audio at a time.

To capture up to 2 channels of audio follow the procedure already described.

To capture more than 2 channels of audio requires you to first Log the clip and then choose the command to Modify Clip Settings.

This process can be achieved in one of two ways:

1   Open the Log and Capture window.

2   Mark 'in' and 'out': points on the clip you wish to capture.

3   Log the clip.

4   Click the clip in the Browser to highlight it.

5   Click the Modify menu and scroll down to Clip Settings.

Control-click the logged clip in the Browser

Alternatively Control click the logged clip in the Browser – this will give you the option to choose Clip Settings.

47

6 Specify the number of channels you wish to capture by clicking the green radio buttons. Green indicates that a particular channel will be captured.

7 Choose if you want channels to be linked together as Stereo Pairs.

Modify Clip Settings

Modify Tracks of Type: **Audio and Video**
     Audio Only
Number of selected offli   Video Only

☑ Video

☑ Audio

Input Channels   8   ☐ Preview

Master Gain ◄⌐⌐⌐⌐⌐⌐⌐⌐⌐⌐▷   1

    1
    2
    3
    4
Toggle Mono or Stereo
    5
    6
    7
    8

Green means the sound from a particular channel will be captured

(Cancel)   (OK)

8 Click OK.

9 Click Batch, bottom right of the Log and Capture window, and Final Cut Pro will now capture the clip and all the audio channels you have specified.

Capturing HDV

There is very little difference when capturing HDV footage to capturing any other footage, however, be aware the Log and Capture window appears more modern and stream-lined.

There are a few differences:

1　By default, when capturing the clips these are broken into separate shots. Think of this as being an auto-DV-Start-Stop-Detect function (refer to page 61). This function can be switched off in the Clip Settings tab of the HDV Log and Capture window.

2　While your HDV footage is captured over Firewire you can only play it back over Firewire as a standard definition DV signal. It is not possible to playback a high definition HDV signal over Firewire.

3　When capturing, the display in the HDV Capture window is widescreen to accommodate the HDV format.

Note: The Capture window when working with HDV is widescreen as is the display while capturing.

49

Log and Transfer

When working with Panasonic P2 media, or Sony SxS cards, the procedure for getting the files into Final Cut Pro is different to working with tape.

Solid-state media, unlike tape, has no moving parts and the files can be accessed in a non-linear fashion. There is no spooling, transfer can take place faster than real-time, there are no dropouts and the media is designed for acquisition but not for archiving. Recording to solid-state media also provides for variable frame-rate recording – known as undercranking and overcranking (terms borrowed from the film world.) This provides for high quality, film-like, slow motion and fast motion.

Panasonic P2 media

As with tape based media one needs to set the Scratch Disks so that Final Cut Pro is told where to store the files.

Sony SxS cards

| 1 | Go to the file menu and choose System Settings. The familiar Scratch Disks window will appear. Select a drive to store your files and follow the procedure already described earlier for setting the Scratch Disks with tape based media. |

Final Cut Pro   File   Edit   View

About Final Cut Pro

User Preferences...   ⌥Q
System Settings...   ⇧Q

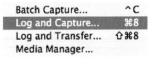

| 2 | Go to the file menu and scroll down to Log and Transfer, located immediately below Log and Capture. |

Batch Capture...   ^C
Log and Capture...   ⌘8
Log and Transfer...   ⇧⌘8
Media Manager...

| 3 | Assuming you have a P2 or SxS card mounted on the desktop of your Mac, you will then be greeted by a visual list of the media on the card. |

The upper left section of the Log and Transfer window provides a clip Browser which will display all of the clips contained on the solid-state card. If you select a clip, you can then play the clip in the Preview window located to the right of the screen. 'In' and 'out' points can be set thus one can define the portion of the clip to be imported, and clips can be named and other details entered.

4 When you have viewed and named the clips highlight and drag clip/clips from the Log and Transfer Browser into the area labeled 'Drag media here.'

Alternatively click 'Add Selection to Queue.'

Import will now take place.

(**Add Selection to Queue**)

If you choose you can also import clips one at a time from the Preview window by clicking on the 'Add Clip to Queue'. If you click on the 'Import Settings' tab you can choose to import audio and video, audio only or video only.

There is a spinning arrow that indicates import in progress. As each clip is imported into FCP it disappears from the clip queue.

Image: Ken Stone (www.kenstone.net)

Essentially importing media from sold-state cards is a remarkably simple process. You can completely skip all the detail, if you choose.

Simply load your P2 card so it is recognized by the Mac and then drag your media from the Browser area into the area labeled 'Drag Media Here.' This is quick and easy and one can then name the files once the clips have been imported into Final Cut Pro.

Importing Music from CD

Films are primarily made up of sound and picture. Much of the sound is recorded at the same time the picture is recorded. When it comes to music, more often than not, this will be sourced from compact disc.

Importing tracks from CD into Final Cut Pro is straightforward. To begin with you need to hide the Final Cut Pro application (press Apple H) and go to the desktop to access the CD.

1   Insert the CD into the Mac's CD/DVD drive. Quit iTunes when it opens.

2   Double click the CD icon on your desktop to open it.

3   Drag the track/s you wish to work with direct from the CD to the desktop – wait while the copy process takes place. You may wish to rename the CD track/s once the copy process is finished.

Once the track or tracks have been copied, you need to go back into Final Cut Pro to import the tracks.

1   Make sure Final Cut Pro is open in front of you.

2   Select the File menu and scroll down to Import. Scroll right and select Files.

Restore Project...

Import   ▶   Files...
Export   ▶   Folder...

3   Navigate to the desktop and locate the track/s you wish to import.

4   Highlight the track or tracks you wish to import. If you want to import more than one track hold down the

Desktop   ▶   1 Audio Track
Documents   ▶   2 Audio Track
Library   ▶   3 Audio Track
Movies   ▶   35mm Film Close U

Apple key and click each of the tracks with your mouse button.

5   Press the blue glowing Choose button.

The CD track/s will now appear in the Browser and these are represented by a speaker icon. Rename the track/s if you choose.

An alternative way to import files into Final Cut Pro is to drag them direct from the desktop into the Browser. This will achieve exactly the same result as using the Import Files command.

It is important now to convert the audio sample rate of the imported track/s to match the rest of the audio in your project.

Converting Audio Sample Rates

It is easy to import CD tracks into Final Cut Pro – the complicated part of the process is to get the CD sample rate to match that of the rest of your project. This is important. Mismatching sample rates can cause a variety of problems including pops, clicks and sync drift.

You will remember DV audio is recorded at either 16 bit – 48 kHz or 12 bit – 32 kHz (refer to page 16). The key to trouble-free audio editing within Final Cut Pro is to make sure that all audio is of the same sample rate. Commercial CDs are recorded at 44.1 kHz. It is therefore advisable to convert the sample rate of the CD track to match the rest of the audio in your project.

1 Highlight the CD audio track which needs to be converted in the Browser.

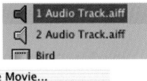

2 Select the File menu, scroll to Export and select Using QuickTime Conversion.

3 Click on the Format bar to reveal a list of options.

4 Select AIFF.

5 Click the Options button to the right.

This will reveal a series of settings. Where it reads Rate – click the two arrows facing in opposite directions. This will reveal a list of audio sample rates.

6 Set the sample rate to 48 kHz and check that 16 bit and Stereo are selected. Click OK.

7 Name the file and save it to hard disk. The conversion process will now take place.

8 Go to the File menu and select Import. Locate the CD file you just exported and import this into the Browser. The sample rate has now been converted to 48 kHz and will now match the rest of your project.

Converting Audio Sample Rates Using QuickTime Pro

Final Cut Pro and Final Cut Studio both come with QuickTime Pro. QuickTime has been described as one of Apple's 'jewels' in the software stakes. It is cross-platform and is used for video production, the creation of Internet content, DVD authoring and even in mobile phone technology. It is not essential that you understand a great deal about QuickTime other than to appreciate if it weren't there video as we know it on the Mac would not exist.

Audio files on CD can be quickly and easily converted from 44.1 kHz to 48 kHz using QuickTime. There are fewer stages involved than with the method described in the previous pages. The advantage of converting directly to disk, using QuickTime, is that you can open up your audio files directly in the QuickTime Player and then convert the file before it is recorded to disk. Therefore, you will only end up with one file which is sampled at 48 kHz.

Before you begin drag the QuickTime Player from your Applications folder onto the Dock for easy access.

Drag the CD Track onto the QuickTime Player

1 Insert the CD into your Mac.

2 Quit iTunes when it opens.

3 Double click the CD on the desktop to open it.

4 Choose an audio track and drag it onto the QuickTime Player on the Dock.

5 Release the audio file and it will open in the QuickTime Player.

6 Go to the File menu, top left of screen and scroll to Export.

7 From the dialogue box which opens choose **Sound to AIFF** and click on the button titled **Options**.

Export: | Sound to AIFF | Options...
Use: | Most Recent Settings |

New Folder   Cancel   Save

The Sound Settings box will now open.

8 Confirm the sample rate is set to 48 kHz; the Sample size needs to be 16 and Channels should be set to Stereo.

9 Save the audio file to a location of your choice.

10 Import the audio file into the Browser of Final Cut Pro or drag directly from the saved location into the Browser.

Sound Settings

Format: Linear PCM

Channels: Stereo (L R)

Rate: 48.000   kHz

☐ Show Advanced Settings

Sample Rate Converter Settings:
Quality: Normal

Linear PCM Settings:
Sample size: 16   bits

☐ Little Endian
☐ Floating Point
☐ Unsigned

Cancel   OK

Once the audio file is accessible in the Browser of Final Cut Pro you can confirm that the sample rate is correct.

1 Control click on the audio file.

2 Scroll to Item Properties and scroll right to Format.

3 Check the audio sample rate listed towards the bottom of the Item Properties window.

At any time you can check the audio sample rate of any of the files in the Browser. It's simply a matter of Control clicking, choosing Item Properties, scrolling to Format and then checking the setting. If sample rates mismatch this can be easily identified and corrected. Export the file from Final Cut Pro using QuickTime Conversion, then re-import the new file into the Browser.

ORGANIZING YOUR FOOTAGE

Final Cut Pro's benefit is that it is more productive.
It allows the editor to get more done.
MICHAEL VITTI
NEW YORK FINAL CUT PRO USER GROUP

Viewing Clips

Now that you have captured your clips you need to be able to view them. This is the first step towards sorting through your footage. To view your material double click any of the clips in the Browser and immediately the clip will open in the Viewer. Press the Space Bar and the clip will play.

The controls in the Viewer window can also be used to play the clip. You can move quickly through the clip using the yellow Scrubber Bar, located below the image in the Viewer. Simply click once with the mouse and move the Scrubber Bar backwards or forwards.

It is also possible to shuttle through the clip using the J K L method. By tapping the 'J' or 'L' key up to five times the speed will increase in increments. Press 'K' or the Space Bar to stop. Press the Space Bar again to play.

To jog through the clip a frame at a time press the horizontal arrow keys located to the right of the Space Bar. The left arrow takes you backwards a frame at a time while the right arrow takes you forward a frame at a time. Hold down the Shift key and press either of the arrow keys and this will move forwards or backwards through the clip a second at a time.

Playing Video through Firewire

When working with video designed to be watched on television it is desirable to play the video signal through a deck or camera and onto a standard television screen. This is because the images on a television screen provide a true representation of the final quality of your finished movie. Otherwise, you will be working exclusively off the computer monitor which provides a different type of picture to that of a television set. Much of the content produced today will be watched over the internet, on iPods, Playstations or on computer screens. However the most popular viewing medium remains television. There would barely be a household in the modern world which does not own at least one TV.

When editing DV footage the deck or camera must be set to receive video through the Firewire cable. A large 6-pin to small 4-pin Firewire cable will link your computer to the Firewire device. You must make sure the correct input is selected if you are using a deck, or, if using a camera, make sure that it is switched to VTR mode. Beyond this the output from the Firewire device needs to be fed into the television set.

Within Final Cut Pro check that the External Video is set to play all frames through Firewire.

1 Choose the View menu found at the top center of the screen.

2 Scroll to video and select All Frames.

The video signal will now play direct from the Mac to your deck or camera and onto the television set.

DV Start/Stop Detection

Back in the old days the film editor would take the workprint when it returned from the lab and cut it into pieces. These pieces were individual shots or sequences of film. The problem with having a huge amount of film on a reel, which had not been broken down into shots, was that it was unwieldy and time consuming to work with. Imagine if the editor of 40 years ago had a machine that would do that part of the process for them.

Well you do have it. Inside of Final Cut Pro is a remarkable feature that will break up long captured clips into individual shots. Each time the record button is pressed on a DV camera a signal is recorded to the tape – another signal is then recorded to tape when the recording stops. Final Cut Pro recognizes this recorded signal and once footage has been captured you can run your footage through what is called Scene Detection. Effectively Scene Detection scans through your footage and breaks it up into individual shots.

Mark	Modify	Sequence
Mark In		i
Mark Out		o
Mark Split		▶
Mark Clip		x
Mark to Markers		⌃A
Mark Selection		⇧A
Select In to Out		⌥A
Set Poster Frame		⌃P

DV Start/Stop Detect

1 Highlight a clip or group of clips in the Browser (a group of clips can be selected by dragging a lasso with your mouse around several clips or by holding down the Apple key while clicking on the individual clips).

2 Select the Mark menu and scroll down to DV Start/Stop Detection – release your mouse button.

3 A progress bar will appear as the clip or clips are scanned by the computer.

Scanning DV Movie(s)

76%

4 Look to the clip(s) you have just scanned. Notice there is a little arrow next to the clip name. Click the arrow and this will reveal a set of pink arrows. Each of these arrows represents a time when the DV camera has started and stopped recording. If you click any of the segments you can then view each of the shots in the Viewer.

DV Start/Stop Detection is a very useful function. If you wish you can capture an entire tape's worth of material and then have the computer break up the footage into individual shots. Effectively the computer does a great deal of sorting through the raw material for you. What it doesn't do is name the individual shots or sort out the good takes from the bad. That is something you must do.

Working with Bins

In the old days before videotape was invented, and certainly before digital cameras and computers were used to acquire and edit productions, a film editor would organize strips of film in an area known as a trim bin. These film strips were hung on a horizontal rack and ordered according to the wishes of the film editor.

While a lot has changed technologically, when working with a non-linear editing system such as Final Cut Pro, it is still crucial to order your material. Otherwise, it soon becomes impossible to track down your shots, particularly if you are working with hours of footage and thousands of clips. Final Cut Pro certainly has the power to handle productions of this magnitude!

To facilitate a simple way of ordering your material it is possible to create what are called bins within the Browser window. Within each of these bins you can store individual clips. The term bin, as you may have guessed, is taken from the era of film editing.

1   To create a new bin select the File menu at the top left of the screen – scroll down to New and select Bin. Alternatively, press Apple B (the Apple button is located immediately left of the Space Bar).

2   In the Browser a box will appear titled Bin 1. This box is clear and different in shape to the clips so there is little likelihood of confusion. You can rename the bin by typing a name immediately after it has been created. Should you wish to rename the bin later, simply click

once on the text area, then pause, and click again in the text area. You can now overtype the title and name the bin whatever you wish. Press return once you have renamed the bin.

Now that you have created and named a bin you can place clips inside it. Clips can be moved, one at a time, by clicking once on the clip and dragging into a bin with the mouse. To select multiple clips use the mouse to drag a lasso around the clips you wish to highlight. Drag the highlighted clips over a bin and release the mouse button. The clips will then be dropped inside the bin.

Highlight Clips and Drag these into a Bin

Several clips can also be selected, one at a time, by holding down the Alt/Option key (located second to the left of the Space Bar) and clicking on each of the clips you wish to highlight. Drag the highlighted clips into the bin and release your mouse button.

To view the contents of a bin:

1 Click the triangle to the left of the bin's title and the contents will be displayed in descending order.

2 Alternatively, double click the bin and a floating window will appear with the bin's contents visible in front of you. To close the floating window click the button at the top left and the bin will return to its original position within the Browser.

You can create as many bins as you like. And you can also store bins within bins. Simply drag a bin over another bin and release your mouse button. The result is a bin stored within a bin.

Items can be moved from one bin to another by highlighting and dragging. Should you wish to move an item from within a bin back to the Browser, you must double click the bin to open it as a floating window and then drag the item or items out of the bin and into the Browser where they will be positioned.

If you want to delete either a clip or a bin highlight the item and press the delete key. Note that the items are only deleted from the Browser and not from your hard drive. Everything inside of Final Cut Pro works by referencing to the original files which exist in the scratch disk folder/s which you set up earlier. Original clips remain stored on the hard disk of your Mac unless you actually go into the hard drive, remove the items and then place them in the trash on the dock. By emptying the trash the items are then deleted.

Working in Icon View

By default Final Cut Pro will display clips in list mode, which means the clips are represented by the names you give to them during the logging process. It can be advantageous to view your clips as icons, or miniature pictures, particularly if you are the sort of person who prefers to work visually. It can be easier to identify a clip by a picture icon, rather than scrolling through an alphabetical list of words.

To view clips in icon mode:

1 Click in the Browser to make the Browser active.

2 Select the View menu at the top of the screen and scroll down to Browser Items.

3 Choose any of the icon views – you will notice it is possible to view as Small,

Medium or Large Icons. The items in the Browser will now be represented by pictures, rather than by words.

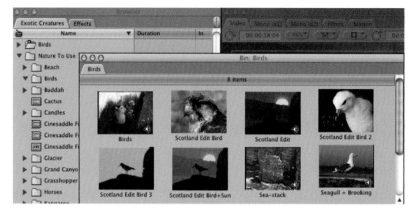

By selecting the Arrange function, found under the View menu, the icons can be lined up by name (alphabetically) or by size.

My preference is to keep the items in the Browser in list view and items inside each of the bins in Icon view. By using this combination one has the advantage of being able to view the material both ways. If one clicks on the arrow to the left of any of the bins, the clips will be displayed in list view; whereas if one double clicks a bin the contents can then be displayed as icons.

Setting Poster Frames

As described, when you work in icon view, each clip is represented visually in the form of a miniature icon. The picture used to represent each of the clips is called the Poster Frame. The Poster Frame is determined by the first frame of the clip.

A problem arises when the first frame of the captured clip is not representative of the shot. Look at the above example. The image on the left does nothing to represent a Seagull, whereas the image on the right says it all.

It is possible to set any image from within the clip to be the Poster Frame.

1   Open the clip into the Viewer and position the Scrubber Bar on the frame you wish to display.

2   Select the Mark menu at the top of the screen and scroll down to Set Poster Frame. Release the mouse button and the image on the thumbnail will now change to that which you have selected.

Mark	Modify	Sequenc
Mark In		i
Mark Out		o
Mark Split		▶
Mark Clip		x
Mark to Markers		^A
Mark Selection		⇧A
Select In to Out		⌥A
Set Poster Frame		^P
DV Start/Stop Detect		

It is also possible to reset the Poster Frame to the first frame of the shot simply by selecting the Clear Poster Frame command which is also found under the Mark menu.

Searching for Clips

Final Cut Pro is a powerful editor capable of referencing to thousands of clips stored on the hard drives of your computer. As the editor you have to know what footage is there and how to get to it. It is all very well to know that it is there somewhere – if you can't find it you are lost.

The most useful database of all is the human mind. An editor will constantly refer to the list in their mind to retrieve a shot ephemerally before actually doing so electronically.

When working on a large project, with hundreds or thousands of separate clips, you need a system to find what you need. Providing you have taken care to label each of your clips in a way that is easy for you to identify with, you will then be able to search for any clip in your project. Apple has made this possible in an extremely simple and elegant way.

To search for a clip:

1   Click once anywhere in the gray area of the Browser.

2   Hold down the Apple key and press the letter F. This will open the Search/Find dialog box. Alternatively, this can be accessed from the Edit menu by scrolling to the Find command.

Find

Search: [Project: Exotic Creatures][⬍]   (**Find Next**)

For: [All Media][⬍]   (**Find All**)

Results: [Replace Find Results][⬍]   (Cancel)

(Less) (**More**)

☐ Omit [Any Column][⬍] [Contains][⬍] helicopter

3 Type the name of a clip or part of the name you wish to search for and then press Find All. All relevant items will then be placed in a bin in front of you.

Find Results

Name
Dramatic Helicopter
Helicopter
Helicopter...
Niagra Falls Helicopter
Niagra Falls Helicopter1
Niagra Falls Helicopter2
Niagra Falls Helicopter3
Niagra Falls Helicopter3
Niagra Falls Helicopter4
Niagra Falls Helicopter4

What would have taken a lot of effort in the past, when working with film or tape, has now been reduced to only a few seconds' work. You still need to rely on your mind to know what you are looking for, however, the difficult work of actually locating the clips has been made very easy. That is assuming you have labelled your clips correctly and that you know what you are looking for in the first place.

Any Column
Name
Duration
In
Out
Media Start
Media End
TC Rate
Tracks
Good (Y/N)

The Search facility within Final Cut Pro can be quite sophisticated. There are many options available beyond the simple method of searching within the Browser as just described. It is possible to search by name, column, through the log notes and a variety of other criteria.

EDITING

What's so good about it is it is uncompromisingly powerful. The most insanely powerful application for under a thousand bucks.
STEVE MARTIN
APPLE CERTIFIED TRAINER

Any film is literally built. Just as a novel will have chapters and subplots, each and every film has an underlying structure. The raw components needed to build the film are planned for in the scripting stage, gathered while filming and structured during editing.

I liken the filmmaking process to making a set of chopsticks from a tree-trunk. An entire tree can be whittled away to leave nothing remaining other than two small pieces of wood – these are the chopsticks. Film or video is the same. A mountain of footage is acquired and throughout the editing process this footage is chopped down to a fraction of its original size to leave a small, yet refined, remnant of the original content.

In simple terms editing is nothing more than putting shots and sounds together. In reality it is much more than this. It is both a technical and a creative process – it is also intuitive. Anyone can string words together, but not everyone is able to write a good story or a good book without a sound knowledge of language. Editing is similar.

There are several key methods of editing with Final Cut Pro. Of these the most important to understand are Insert and Overwrite Editing. While there are other methods available such as Replace Editing, Fit to Fill and Superimpose, provided you understand Insert and Overwrite Editing you will be able to edit any production.

Let me stress, the key to editing with Final Cut Pro lies in the difference between Insert and Overwrite Editing and when to use one or the other. Beyond this, you must understand how to control audio in relation to these two ways of editing. Once you have this clear in your mind you are well on the way to mastering Final Cut Pro. You will then have the technical knowledge to make a film that is fully professional and equal to whatever you watch on TV or see at the cinema. I'm not kidding here. You will be able to edit anything from a thirty second commercial to a feature film.

Insert and Overwrite Editing

Think of the old days when film was edited in a cutting room. The editor would take two pieces of film, line them up in a splicer and join them together. As more pieces of film were cut together a Sequence was formed. As more Sequences were crafted these were joined together to build completed scenes until finally titles and effects were added. Once all the scenes were completed the final result was a finished film.

When putting the pieces of film together the editor had two choices: either a piece of film was added to the shots already cut together and therefore the overall length of the Sequence was increased, or a piece of film was placed into the Sequence and a corresponding amount of film, the same in length, removed – thus the overall duration did not change. These two choices are what Insert and Overwrite Editing are all about.

When you build your movie in Final Cut Pro you edit various shots together. Whenever these shots are put together you must decide whether you are adding a shot to a Sequence and therefore increasing the overall length of the movie, or, whether you wish to simply replace a section with another shot previously not included (thus keeping the Sequence the same in length).

When editing with a non-linear system such as Final Cut Pro the editor has a lot more in common with the film editors of yesterday than the tape editors of recent times.

Getting Started with Editing

1   Check that you have a Sequence open. If you can see the Timeline in front of you then a Sequence is already open. Your Sequences are stored in the Browser, the same area where your clips and bins are kept. If a Sequence is not open double click a Sequence in the Browser and the Timeline will appear.

2   Choose a clip from the Browser and double click it – this will load the clip into the Viewer (you may have to open one of your bins if you have filed away all of your clips).

3   With your clip loaded in the Viewer scrub through it. You can do this either by using the Scrubber Bar, or by using 'J' to scrub backwards or 'L' to scrub forwards (tap either of these keys in increments to speed up the rate of scrubbing). Use the Space Bar to start or stop.

4   Choose a point in the clip where you wish to mark an edit point. Press the 'i' key to mark the 'in' point.

5   Choose the point where you wish to mark the end point of the clip – this will be the 'out' point. Press 'o' to mark the 'out' point.

The procedure for marking 'in' and 'out' points is the same as that you already experienced during the logging process.

Once you have marked the 'in' and 'out' points you are now ready to edit the shot into the Sequence. There should be no shots in the Sequence at this stage and therefore the Timeline will be empty.

Make sure the Scrubber Bar is positioned at the beginning of the Timeline. To do this click anywhere near the numbers in the light shade of gray at the top of the Timeline. You will now see the yellow Scrubber Bar with a vertical line extending from top to bottom. Drag the Scrubber Bar along this light gray area and position it at the beginning of the Sequence (all the way to the left). Alternatively, press the Home key on your keyboard and this will have the same effect.

6 Click with your mouse in the center of the clip that you have loaded into the Viewer. A small transparent box will appear where you click. While still holding the mouse button, drag the cursor over the Canvas (the window to the right of the Viewer).

A selection of options will appear. The top option is Insert, followed by Overwrite, then Replace, Fit to Fill and Superimpose. At this stage we are only concerned with the first two options: Insert and Overwrite.

7   Move the cursor, with the transparent box, over the Insert button (marked yellow). Release your mouse button. Look to the Timeline and notice there is now a single block positioned at the beginning. This is the first shot of your Sequence.

8   Repeat the above process with another shot. Double click a shot to load it into the Viewer and mark the 'in' and 'out' points. Click on the shot in the Viewer, drag this over the Canvas and release it over the yellow Insert button. You now have two shots in the Timeline.

9   Edit several more shots together – choose between five and ten shots. When you have cut these together, use the Scrubber Bar in the Timeline to move back and forth through the Sequence. Position the Scrubber Bar at the beginning of the Sequence and press the Space Bar. The shots will play in the Canvas and onto your television monitor – assuming you are plugged into a deck/camera and video is playing through Firewire. If video is not playing through Firewire check that All Frames is selected under External Video found under the View menu.

Note: you can also scrub through your Sequence in the Canvas by using the Scrubber Bar at the bottom of the Canvas. The Canvas and the Timeline are linked in that the Timeline is a graphical representation of all the shots edited together in the Canvas. The Timeline shows individual clips as blocks, whereas the Canvas shows the shots as moving images.

Distinguishing between Insert/Overwrite

In the Timeline you should now have several shots edited together. Position the Scrubber Bar in the Timeline at the beginning of the Sequence. Press the upward arrow on your keyboard (located to the right of the Space Bar) and you will find you are now able to skip forward between each of the shots. Press the downward arrow and you will find you can skip backwards through your shots, one by one.

     Skip Forwards

     Skip Backwards

Now, position the Scrubber Bar in the middle of the Sequence.

1   Open a shot in the Viewer and mark the 'in' and 'out' points.

2   Drag this shot over to the Canvas, however, this time, instead of releasing it over the Insert button, position it over the Overwrite button (marked red). Now release your mouse button.

3   The shot will be edited into the Timeline – but it will not push all of the other shots in front of it further along in the Sequence. Instead, it will write over a portion of the Sequence beginning where your Scrubber Bar is positioned.

If it is not obvious that this has happened it may be necessary to condense the overall spread of the shots on the Timeline. To do this, look to the bottom of the Timeline and find the slider bar with two ribbed ends. Drag either of these ribbed ends and you will see that the Timeline can be expanded or contracted. This does not affect the length of your movie in any way. What it does is to affect the display of your Sequence.

Ribbed End

Expanded View of Timeline

Press **Shift** + **Z** to contract the Timeline so that it will fit on the entire screen in front of you.

Contracted View of Timeline

This is very useful when you have a Sequence that is long and you wish to be able to view the entire Sequence on the screen in front of you. It is also useful when you wish to expand the Sequence for fine control to allow precise positioning of the Scrubber Bar.

To make completely clear the difference between Insert and Overwrite Editing it is advisable to condense the Timeline so the entire contents are visible on screen. You will then be able to determine the type of edit: if the Timeline has been made longer, you have performed an Insert Edit; if the length does not change you have performed an Overwrite Edit.

To be able to see the difference between Insert and Overwrite Editing:

1 Position the Scrubber Bar on a shot change in the middle of the Timeline.

2 Open a shot in the Viewer and mark an 'in' and 'out' point.

3 Drag the shot from the Viewer to the Canvas and position it over the Insert button. Observe the Timeline as you release the mouse button and notice all other shots get pushed further along the Sequence.

4 Hold down the Apple key and press the letter 'Z'. This will undo the action you have just performed.

77

5   Repeat the procedure of dragging the shot from the Viewer to the Canvas, however, this time, release it over the Overwrite button. It should be apparent that a different effect has taken place. The shots in the Sequence are not pushed further along the Timeline – they all stay in exactly the same position. What has happened is that the shot you have just edited into the Sequence has written over a portion of the Timeline. The length is determined by the 'in' and 'out' points in the Viewer.

If you look at the top left of the Viewer you can see the duration of the shot you are working with. This is measured in seconds and frames. If you change the position of either the 'in' or 'out' points Final Cut Pro will calculate the new duration.

Note: it is not necessary to drag the video from the Viewer to the Canvas to perform an Insert or Overwrite Edit. If you prefer, mark the 'in' and 'out' points in the Viewer and press either the yellow or red buttons at the bottom of the Canvas. Providing you remember that yellow is for Insert and red is for Overwrite then these functions can be accessed in this way.

Three Point Editing

So far we have only marked 'in' and 'out' points in the Viewer with the positioning of the Scrubber Bar determining where the Insert or Overwrite Edit will be edited in the Timeline. It is also possible to enter the 'in' and 'out' points directly into the Timeline. Simply position the Scrubber Bar where you want to mark the 'in' point and press 'i' and similarly press 'o' where you want to mark the 'out' point.

By marking a single 'in' point in the Viewer you can then perform an Insert or Overwrite Edit. The positioning and duration of the edit is determined by the 'in' and 'out' points marked in the Timeline.

Viewer

'In' Point   'Out' Point

Timeline: Sequence 3 in Exotic Creatures

01:00:04:00   01:0 'In' Point   'Out' Point

Face in the snow | Tibetan | Bud   Timeline   's in Snow | Conten

Face in the snow | Tibetan | Buddhah Carving | Yaks in Snow | Contemplatio

Face in the snow | Tibetan | Buddhah Carving | Yaks in Snow | Contemplatio

It is also possible to mark the 'in' and 'out' points in the Canvas.

What is being illustrated here is known as **Three Point Editing**. Essentially, all editing in Final Cut Pro works according to the Three Point Editing system. Even if it appears that only two points have been marked, the positioning of the Scrubber Bar in the Timeline serves as the third point.

It is important to be aware that whatever points are marked in the Timeline will be reflected in the Canvas and vice versa. The Timeline and Canvas are intimately related at all times – they are in no way independent of each other.

It may be clear at this stage just how closely the Viewer and Canvas mimic a traditional two-machine editing suite. If one forgets about the Timeline for the moment, all that is taking place is marking 'in' and 'out' points in the Viewer and/or Canvas. This is the same process as marking 'in' and 'out' points in a two-machine edit suite with a source VTR and a record VTR.

Other Editing Options

So far we have looked at Insert and Overwrite Editing. You will have noticed other options can be chosen when one drags a clip from the Viewer to the Canvas.

Replace

Fit to Fill

Superimpose

Replace Editing – this is used to overwrite a shot into the Timeline, from the Viewer, with the duration being determined by the shot which already exists in the Timeline. By marking an 'in' point in both the Viewer and Timeline/Canvas, the shot being edited will match the duration of the shot being replaced in the Timeline. There is no need to mark an 'out' point.

Fit to Fill – Four points need to be marked to achieve a Fit to Fill edit: an 'in' and 'out' point in the Viewer and an 'in' and 'out' point in the Timeline or Canvas. The shot in the Viewer will then be either sped up or slowed down to fit into the space of the shot which is being overwritten in the Timeline. The overwritten section of the Timeline will then need to be rendered (dealt with later).

Superimpose – This is used for creating a second layer of video. When using this type of edit a shot is edited from the Viewer to the second video track in the Timeline. No apparent result will be noticed, other than that of an overwrite edit, unless the edited shot is reduced in size, effectively creating a picture in picture. If the opacity of the clip were to be adjusted then a superimposition would be the result.

Modifying 'In' and 'Out' Points

If you wish to clear 'in' or 'out' points there are several ways to achieve this.

1   Select the Mark menu at the top of the screen.

2   Scroll down and choose the relevant option: clear 'in' and 'out', clear 'in' or clear 'out'.

Keyboard shortcuts can be used to perform these functions. Hold down the Alt/Option button (two keys to the left of the Space Bar).

Alt/Option + x	**Clear 'in' and 'out'**
Alt/Option + i	**Clear 'in'**
Alt/Option + o	**Clear 'out'**

By holding down the Control key and clicking in the area where one scrolls with the Scrubber Bar, in either the

Mark   Modify   Sequ

Mark In
Mark Out
Mark Split
Mark Clip
Mark to Markers
Mark Selection
Select In to Out
Set Poster Frame

DV Start/Stop Detec
Audio Peaks

Clear In and Out

Clear In and Out
Clear In
Clear Out
Clear Split   ▶

Mark In
Mark Out

Viewer, Canvas or Timeline, a contextual menu will appear. 'In' and 'out' points can be set or cleared by choosing the relevant command.

It is also possible to alter the 'in' or 'out' points by dragging or repositioning.

1   Click on the 'in' or 'out' point symbol in the Viewer, Canvas or Timeline and drag it to where you want it to be repositioned.

2   Alternatively, position the Scrubber Bar where you want the 'in' or 'out' point to be and press 'i' or 'o'. The 'in' or 'out' point is then repositioned and the previous 'in' or 'out' point is effectively deleted.

Directing the Flow of Audio/Video

The editing that we have done so far has involved editing video and audio at the same time. To produce a professional film one needs to be able to edit video and audio separately. This is easy to achieve with Final Cut Pro and as with many of the editing functions there is more than one way to go about it.

Look to the left of the Timeline and you will notice that where each track is labelled V1 (video 1) and A1 and A2 (audio 1 and 2) there is also a lower-case v1, a1 and a2 symbol. I refer to these as break-off tabs. If you click these tabs you will notice that they break away from the fixed video and audio symbols.

This is a simple patch facility which enables you to quickly and easily direct the flow of audio and video.

1   Click the break-off tab, v1, next to the capitalized V1 symbol.

2 You will notice it immediately slides slightly to the left, and is effectively broken away from the fixed V1 symbol. This means that track is inactive for editing.

Click the Break-off Tabs to Target or Disable Tracks for Editing

3 Do the same to the break-off tabs next to A1 and A2. The lower-case tabs will slide to the left of the capitalized A1 and A2 symbols.

Audio Flows to Tracks 2 & 3   **Audio Flows to Tracks 3 & 4**

By clicking again on any of these tabs they will slide to the right and rejoin with the symbols to the right, indicating that those tracks are now targeted, or active, for editing.

Now, click one of the audio break-off tabs a1 and slide it to track A3. Release your mouse button and you will see that it remains joined to the new track where you have repositioned it. Repeat the procedure again with the audio break-off tab a2 so that it attaches to A4.

Wherever the break-off tab is positioned indicates that audio or video will flow to that particular track. If a tab is disconnected, nothing will flow to the track. The tabs toggle back and forth as they are clicked, indicating that a particular track is targeted or not targeted for editing. The tabs can be moved from one track to another by sliding, or by clicking, to allow you to direct the flow of audio or video.

For example, if you have V1 connected and A1 and A2 disconnected, then video will be edited across into the Timeline and audio will be restricted. In contrast, should A1 and A2 be connected and V1 disconnected – then only audio will be edited and the video will remain unaffected.

In simple terms, whatever is connected will be edited into the Timeline and whatever is disconnected will remain unaffected.

Locking Tracks

An alternative way to edit video and audio independently of each other is by locking or unlocking tracks. This provides a very simple and effective way to prevent either audio and video or a combination of both from flowing through to a particular track or series of tracks. It is as simple as locking the track or tracks that you do not wish to alter.

Look to the left-hand side of the Timeline and you will see there is a single video track and four audio tracks. This is the default number of video and audio tracks which Final Cut Pro provides you with when you launch the program.

To the immediate right of the V1, A1 and A2 symbols are little locks. Click on the locks and notice the track or tracks become grayed out.

This means that when you edit material from the Viewer to the Canvas, and into the Timeline, the only part of the Timeline which is affected is that which is not locked (or not grayed out).

To lock a track prevents it from being affected during editing. The only way to reactivate the track is to unlock it. This is done by clicking the lock on the left-hand side of the Timeline. Once the track is unlocked it no longer appears grayed out.

The usual rules regarding Insert and Overwrite Edits apply.

Video 1 Locked Audio 1 & 2 Unlocked

Video 1 Unlocked Audio 1 & 2 Locked

Adding and Deleting Tracks

Final Cut Pro allows you to work with up to 99 layers of video and audio tracks. The default setup is a single video track and four audio tracks.

There are two ways to add or delete video and audio tracks to your project.

1 Select the Sequence menu and scroll down to either Insert Tracks or Delete Tracks.

2 A menu will appear giving

you the option to choose the number and type of tracks you wish to add or delete. You need to specify where these tracks are to appear in the Timeline by clicking the button options.

An alternative and easier method is to Control click in the gray area to the left of any of the tracks which already exist. A menu will open giving you the choice to either add or delete a track. You can Control click above, below or to the left of the tracks in the Timeline to open up the contextual menu which allows you to add or delete tracks.

Essential Editing Tools

A very important part of the interface that we have not dealt with so far is the Toolbar. With the layout I use this is positioned to the left of the Timeline. However, it really doesn't matter where it sits on the screen providing you can readily access it.

There are nine tools available, however, generally, I use only five of these for most editing tasks. There are also other tools hidden in the submenus within the Toolbar giving a total of 22 options in all.

Pointer (Select Item)

Edit Selection

Arrow (Select Track)

Roll Edit

Slip Edit

Razorblade

Magnifier

Crop

Pen Tool

 Pointer (Select Item) – I call this the home tool – this is the tool I always have selected during the editing process. The Pointer is used for selecting and moving clips around in the Timeline. If I need to access the functions of the other tools I will choose another tool, use it, and then click on the Pointer again. By always having the Pointer selected you know where you are at all times.

Arrow (Select Track) – this is used for selecting individual or multiple tracks, or the entire contents of the Timeline.

Razorblade – used for cutting clips into pieces. Great for trimming edits.

 Magnifying Glass – most useful for expanding and reducing the Timeline. Useful for homing in on the exact part of a clip you wish to work with.

 Pen Tool – essential for adjusting audio levels. Also used for adding keyframes, thus allowing you to plot points over time. Useful for creating effects and adjusting video levels.

It is essential to understand how these tools work in order to edit efficiently. While shots can be strung together without ever touching the tools, in order to be able to trim edits, move shots around, home in on an exact part of a c lip with absolute accuracy and to adjust clip levels and mix audio, one must be able to grasp these tools and how they can be used in combination with each other.

Undo/Redo

As your skills develop and you experiment with the facilities in front of you there will be times when you will get ahead of yourself and you will need to backtrack a few stages.

This is easy to achieve in the form of undo. It is also useful to be able to redo any of the actions you have performed.

At any time an edit can be undone by holding down the Apple key and pressing 'Z'. To perform a redo command press Apple + Shift + Z.

Apple + Z – Undo Action   **Apple + Shift Z – Redo Action**

Multiple levels of undo can be achieved by pressing **Apple 'Z'** several times. Similarly, press **Apple Shift 'Z'** as many times as you wish to perform multiple redos. This ability to undo and redo is particularly useful when comparing changes in different edits. The number of levels of undo/redo can be set in User Preferences found under the Final Cut Pro menu located top left of screen. The default amount is 10 levels of undo/redo. This can be set to a maximum of 99.

Linked/Unlinked Selection

By default your audio and video are locked together. This means clips positioned in the Timeline will be married together in a similar way to film images and magnetic sound-striped tape running together in a synchronizer or a projector.

To illustrate the meaning of Linked Selection make sure you have selected the Pointer from the Toolbar. Check that you have several clips in the Timeline.

1 Point your cursor at a clip in the Timeline and click once. The clip is now highlighted.

2 While still holding down your mouse button, slide this clip to the right or left. Notice that both the audio and video move together.

3 Release the clip you are moving over one of the clips in the Timeline and the video and audio will overwrite the clip over which it is positioned.

4 Press Apple 'Z' and the Overwrite Edit will be undone. The clip will return to its previous position.

5 Click once on the green symbol which resembles a diagonal figure 8 inside a box, located top right of the Timeline. The symbol will turn gray and white to represent that Linked Selection is turned off.

01:00:08:00   01:00:10:00

Contemplation 2

Contemplation 2

Contemplation 2

Linked Selection can also be accessed from the Edit menu at the top of the screen.

Scroll down to Linked Selection; if there is a tick, this means Linked Selection is on; no tick and it is switched off. Linked and Unlinked Selection toggles on and off when accessed through the menu.

With Linked Selection switched off repeat the procedure of selecting a video clip. Slide the video to the right and observe that while the video moves, the audio stays where it is. Conversely, select the audio and you can move this without affecting the video.

Edit	View	Mark	Mc
Undo			
Redo			
Cut			
Copy			
Paste			
Clear			
Duplicate			
Paste Insert			
Paste Attributes...			
Remove Attributes...			
Select All			
Deselect All			
✓ **Linked Selection**			

**Video Moved
Independent of Video**

**Audio Moved
Independent of Video**

To select more than one track at a time hold down the Shift key, while using the Pointer tool, and items can be grouped together. Release the Shift key and the grouped items can be moved and repositioned wherever you wish.

To switch Linked Selection back on, click once on the white circles on the top right-hand side of the Timeline. These will turn green indicating that Linked Selection is switched on – this will apply even if you have moved video and/or audio independently of each other.

Note: an identical effect to linking or unlinking can be achieved by locking your tracks. Simply lock the tracks you do not wish to alter and then slide the video or audio of the clip you wish to move. Even though Linked Selection may still be turned on a locked track or tracks will override the link.

Moving Edits in the Timeline

You may have noticed when you use the Pointer tool to slide a clip to a different location the effect is that of an Overwrite Edit. It is also possible to move edits around in the Timeline, using the Pointer tool, and at the same time perform an Insert Edit.

To perform an Insert Edit within the Timeline it is crucial to press the keys in the correct order.

1   Using the Pointer tool highlight the clip you wish to move and release your mouse button.

2   Press and hold down the Alt/Option key and click once again with the Pointer tool on the clip you wish to move. Reposition the clip by dragging and release your mouse button at the point where you want the clip to be inserted in the Timeline.

This time the result is that of an Insert Edit. The clip you have moved is repositioned and all edits in front of it move forward in the Timeline.

You may notice that the clip has been inserted where you specified in the Timeline and that it also remains in its original position.

To remove the original clip, highlight it and press the delete key. This deletes the clip from the Timeline and leaves a gap where it previously existed.

Gap Where Clip Has Been Deleted

To get rid of the gap hold down the Control key and click in the gap with your cursor – this opens a dialog box with several options – select Close Gap and the gap will disappear.

Control Click in the Gap to Reveal
Contextual Menu

Fill with Slug

The Gap Has Now Been Closed

Note: you can actually delete a clip and close the gap at the same time by highlighting a clip – hold down the shift key and at the same time press delete.

Most Apple keyboards have an additional Delete key to the right of the standard Delete key. Press this key and the close gap function is performed with a single keystroke.

Selecting Multiple Items in the Timeline

You will now be well aware that a clip in the Timeline can be selected by clicking once with the Pointer tool. If you wish to select more than one clip hold down the Shift key while you highlight each of the clips. So long as you continue to hold down the Shift key you can then select as many clips as you wish. These can then be moved within the Timeline using the Overwrite or Insert method.

Another way to select multiple items is to use the Arrow tool. By clicking once and holding, this tool can be extended to reveal various options.

Extended View of Arrow Tool

The Arrow tool is useful for deleting or copying large portions of the Timeline. Simply use the method described below to highlight those clips you wish to work with.

1   Click once to select the horizontal Arrow tool.

2   Your cursor now becomes a horizontal arrow. Use this horizontal arrow and click in the middle of the Timeline. All the clips forward of the arrow will now appear highlighted.

3   Press Delete and the highlighted section will disappear.

4   Press Apple 'Z' to undo the effect.

To copy the selected items repeat the procedure and this time instead of pressing Delete press Apple 'C' – or go to the Edit menu at the top of your screen and scroll down to Copy.

It is then possible to paste these items anywhere in the Timeline.

1   Select the Pointer tool.

2   Place the Scrubber Bar at the position in the Timeline where you wish to Insert or Overwrite the shots you have just copied.

3   Go to the Edit menu at the top of the screen. Select Paste to perform an Overwrite Edit on the section you have copied or select Paste Insert to perform an Insert Edit.

If you click the Toolbar and hold the horizontal arrow down with your mouse the Toolbar will extend to reveal other options within the arrow's capabilities. You can select a horizontal arrow which points backwards rather than forwards and thus select the contents of a track in the reverse direction; you can also select an arrow which points in both directions, allowing you to quickly and easily select the entire contents of an individual track or everything in the Timeline (providing Linked Selection is switched on). You can also select a double arrow, forwards or backwards, which has the effect of selecting all tracks in the direction of the arrows regardless of whether Linked Selection is switched on or off.

 Selects Track/s in a Forward Direction

 Selects Track/s in a Reverse Direction

 Selects Track/s in Both Directions

 Selects all Tracks in a Forward Direction Regardless of Whether Linked Selection is Switched On or Off

Selects all Tracks in a Reverse Direction Regardless of Whether Linked Selection is Switched On or Off

Cut, Copy, Paste

When using Final Cut Pro shots can be cut, copied or pasted using the conventions used in most word processors. These functions can be accessed from the Edit menu at the top of the screen.

To copy or paste a section from the Timeline is easy:

1   Highlight one or more clips in the Timeline and select Copy or Cut using the Edit menu at the top of your screen – or use the shortcuts Apple X (Cut) or Apple C (Copy).

2   Go to the Edit menu at the top of your screen and select either Paste (Apple V) to perform an Overwrite Edit, or Paste Insert (Shift V) to perform an Insert Edit of the copied or cut material.

Paste Insert (Shift V) is an extremely useful function, not found in word processors. As described above, to perform an Insert Edit select Paste Insert, while to perform an Overwrite Edit use Paste.

Snapping and Skipping between Shots

It is easy to skip between shots in the Timeline by dragging the Scrubber Bar which sticks to each of the edit points. If you have a crowded Timeline you may wish to turn this facility off as it can make it difficult to position the Scrubber Bar with accuracy.

Pressing the letter 'N' and snapping toggles on or off. You can also select the green symbol at the extreme top right of your Timeline to achieve the same result.

You can also skip between shots by using the vertical or horizontal arrows on your keyboard – up for forwards, down for backwards. Each press of these arrows will skip past one clip at a time.

The Razorblade Tool

My favorite tool in Final Cut Pro is the Razorblade. This tool is used for cutting clips into smaller pieces and is great for trimming a long shot into a smaller shot or shots.

It is often useful to use the Razorblade in conjunction with the Magnifier tool. By using the Magnifier you can zoom in on a clip or series of clips for greater accuracy when trimming with the Razorblade.

1   Play your Sequence in the Timeline. When you see a shot you would like to trim press the Space Bar to pause playback.

2   Click on the Razorblade tool – your cursor now becomes a Razorblade. Alternatively, press the letter 'B' to select the Razorblade tool.

3   Position the Razorblade where you wish to cut the shot in the Timeline. The Razorblade will automatically be drawn to each edit point providing you have Snapping switched on. If you find the Snapping facility to be impeding your accuracy then switch it off (press the letter 'N'). The Razorblade will also be drawn to the Scrubber Bar. It is therefore useful to position the Scrubber Bar at the exact point where you wish to perform a cut and then position the Razorblade accordingly.

4 Click once to make a cut at the point where the Razorblade is positioned. The track to which the cut applies is determined by whether or not the tracks are linked.

	01:00:06:00		01:00:08:
e snow	Tibetan	Yaks in Snow	Con
v	Tibetan	Yaks in Snow	Contempl:
v	Tibetan	Yaks in Snow	Contempl:

5 Select the Pointer tool and highlight the portion of the shot you wish to remove.

6 Press Shift Delete or press the Delete key to the right of the main keyboard area. This will remove the shot you have highlighted and close the resulting gap at the same time. If you wish to leave a gap only press Delete.

Should you happen to have Linked Selection switched off then the Razorblade will only cut through a single track at a time.

If you wish to cut through all tracks, regardless of whether Linked Selection is on or off, then you need to select the Double Razorblade. This is done by holding your mouse button and clicking on the Razorblade tool – scroll across to select the Double Razorblade. The Double Razorblade will cut through all your tracks even if Linked Selection is switched off. The Double Razorblade can also be selected by pressing the letter 'B' twice in quick succession.

If you wish to heal a cut made by the Razorblade it is possible to perform what is called a Join Through Edit.

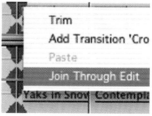

1 Control click on the cut made by the Razor-blade. This will bring up a contextual menu.

2 Select Join Through Edit and release your mouse button. The cut will now be healed.

Note: The Razorblade does not cut through tracks which are locked. You need to switch off the locks for the Razorblade to work.

The Magnifier Tool

If you find it hard to be accurate when positioning the Scrubber Bar or Razorblade then you need to expand the Timeline. This is achieved by pulling on the ribbed ends of the Slider tool at the bottom of the Timeline, or by using the Magnifier tool.

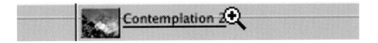

The main difference between the Magnifier tool and the Slider tool is that the Magnifier tool is used to zoom in on a specific section of the Timeline. By using this tool the exact area one wants to magnify will get larger with each press of the button. When using the Slider tool the overall spread of the Timeline is increased or reduced, but not necessarily the specific area you wish to focus in on. The Magnifier is far more accurate.

1 Click once on the Magnifier tool in the Toolbar – your cursor becomes a magnifying glass.

2 Position the magnifying glass over the area of the Timeline you wish to enlarge. Click with the mouse and the Timeline will expand – click again and it expands further. You can continue expanding the Timeline until you are able to work with the individual frames.

3 To contract the Timeline when using the Magnifier press the Alt key and a minus symbol will appear, indicating that the

Magnifier will contract the Timeline. Alternatively, click on the Magnifier in the Toolbar and select the minus Magnifier.

The Magnifier tool can also be selected by pressing the letter 'Z'.

Bringing Clips Back into Sync

Due to the nature of Insert Editing and Overwrite Editing, along with the fact that you can lock/unlock your tracks or activate/deactivate tracks through the break-off tabs, it is inevitable that at some stage your video and audio will get out of sync. Fortunately, Apple has made it very easy to bring items back into sync.

If items are pushed out of sync a red box will appear at the beginning of the clip in the Timeline where the sync trouble has occurred. The red box, which appears in both the video and audio tracks, will have a figure indicating the amount of sync slippage.

To bring the items back into sync:

1   Hold down the Control key and click inside the red box where the numeric value of sync drift is displayed. Control clicking in the red box brings up a dialog box with two possible options.

2   Select Slip into Sync or Move into Sync and release the mouse button. The item or items selected will now be brought back into sync.

Move actually moves the edit in the Timeline, whereas Slip slides it within the parameters of the existing clip.

It is also possible to manually slide the audio or video back into sync.

1 Make sure Linked Selection is turned off and Snapping is turned on. Having Snapping turned on will ensure that the out of sync items will be drawn to the correct sync points.

2 Highlight the item/s you wish to move and drag these so that the out of sync items line up at the beginning of each clip. When you release the mouse button the red box disappears and sync has been restored. If the red box is still visible move the clip again until you find the sync point.

Creating New Sequences

Final Cut Pro is particularly flexible in that you can have many Sequences open at a time. To have multiple Sequences open means that you have access to more than one Timeline – this is most useful for building various sections of a film which can be later joined together using the Cut, Copy, Paste and the Paste Insert functions. Think of having multiple Sequences as like having several different film reels each containing separate edited scenes or parts of a movie.

Multiple Sequences are tiled with cascading tabs from left to right. These tabs are displayed in both the Timeline and Canvas. Click on any of the tabs to flip between the Sequences. The Sequences can be renamed by overtyping the name in the Browser. The label on each of the tabs will then be updated.

1   To create a new Sequence click once inside the Browser. Hold the Apple key and press the letter 'N'. A new

File	Edit	View	Mark	Modify	Sequenc

New	▶	Sequence
New Project	⇧⌘N	Bin
Open...	⌘O	Offline Clip
Open Recent	▶	
Close Window	⌘W	

Sequence will then appear. Another way to create a new Sequence is to select the File menu (top left of screen). Scroll down to New Sequence and release the mouse button. A new Sequence will appear in the Browser.

2   Double click on any Sequence in the Browser to open it. Several Sequences can be opened at any one time. It is possible to rename Sequences at any stage by highlighting the Sequence icon in the Browser and overtyping.

▶ 📁 Clips
📹 Hunting
📹 Man-made Areas
📹 Mountains of Nepal
📹 Sequence 25
📹 Wild Creatures

Subclips

One of the easiest and most useful functions available in Final Cut Pro is the Make Subclip command. A subclip is part of a larger clip – it is therefore possible to have a long clip and to break this clip into many smaller pieces which can be individually named.

1   Open a clip into the Viewer.

2   Mark an 'in' and 'out' point – this will define the beginning and end of the subclip.

3   Go to the Modify menu – select the Make Subclip command.

4   In the Browser a new icon will appear – the name will be that of the clip you have opened in the Viewer with the word Subclip after the title.

Modify	Sequence	E
Make Subclip		
Remove Subclip Limi

▼ 📁 Mountains
   🎬 Contemplation
   🎬 Contemplation Subclip
   🎬 Mountain

Once you have your subclips in the Browser you can organize them into bins in the same way as you would with clips. The subclips can then be edited into the Timeline and worked with in the same way as clips.

Freeze Frame

When working with NTSC video each second is made up of 29.97 individual frames; when working in PAL each second is made up of 25 frames. It is a simple procedure to freeze any of these frames and create what is known as a Freeze Frame.

1   Position the Scrubber Bar on the frame you wish to freeze in either the Timeline or the Viewer.

2   Select the Modify menu at the top of the screen and scroll down to Make Freeze Frame.

Modify	Sequence	Effects
Make Subclip		⌘U
Remove Subclip Limits		
Make Independent Clip		
Make Freeze Frame		⇧N

3   Release your mouse button and the Freeze Frame with 'in' and 'out' points marked is positioned in the Viewer. By default a 12 second freeze is created (this can be set in User Preferences found under the Final Cut Pro menu).

4   If you want the Freeze Frame to be accessible within the Browser then drag the frame from the Viewer into the first column of the Browser. The Freeze Frame is represented by a graphic symbol within the Browser when viewed in list mode.

Drag the Freeze from the Viewer

If you find a Freeze Frame to be jittery you need to add the deinterlace filter. An explanation of using filters is described later in the Effects section.

Match Frame Editing

In on-line edit suites it is often necessary to perform a function known as Match Frame Editing. This means a specific frame is cued on a record machine, and an identical frame is cued on a source machine. By editing from the source VTR to the record VTR a seamless edit is performed. This facility was particularly useful in linear, multi-machine edit suites, before non-linear technology existed, when the editor did their best to minimize dubbing shots from one tape to another.

Match Frame Button

Match Frame Editing is still relevant in non-linear edit suites, such as Final Cut Pro, although it can be used for different reasons. It can be extremely useful to be able to find an exact frame in a Sequence with absolute accuracy. This technique can be used to locate a clip quickly and to put this clip into the Viewer for easy access.

To achieve a Match Frame Edit:

1 Place the Scrubber Bar in the Timeline on the frame you wish to match to in the Viewer.

2 Press the 'F' key on the keyboard or press the Match Frame button in the Canvas.

3 The frame on which you are positioned in the Timeline will now be displayed in both the Viewer and the Canvas.

4 By marking the 'in' and 'out' points in the Viewer and (if required) the Timeline, you can perform a seamless frame accurate edit. This is what is known as Match Frame Editing.

Note: if you are working with many layers of video or many audio tracks, and you wish to match frame to a particular layer or track, then you need to use the Auto-Select Toggle facility. This is located to the right of the locks in each track in the Timeline.

| Match to V1 | Match to V2 | Match to V3 |

The Match Frame function, by default, will match to the base layer. Switch off the Auto-Select on the base layer and the Match Frame facility will then match to the second layer of video. Switch off the second layer of video and you can then match to the third layers of video, and so forth.

The same applies to the audio tracks in descending order.

While it may not be immediately clear exactly how useful Match Frame Editing is, there are many instances where it can make the difference between being able to successfully create an effect or not. It is also the easiest method of finding a shot without having to look through the Browser and all of the bins. Simply line up the Scrubber Bar in the Timeline – press the 'F' key – and the shot is immediately matched to.

The Positioning of the Scrubber Bar in the Timeline is Matched to in the Viewer

Slow/Fast Motion

No editing program would be complete without being able to perform slow motion or fast motion to a clip or series of clips. Final Cut Pro performs admirably in this area, giving the freedom to slow images down to 1% or to speed images up in excess of 1000%. It is also possible to play images in reverse.

| 1 | Click once in the Timeline and highlight the shot you wish to slow down or speed up. |
| 2 | Go to the Modify menu at the top of the screen and scroll down to Speed. |

Constant Speed ⬍

Duration: 00:00:01:10

Speed: 50 percent

3 Enter a percentage value to set the speed you wish the shot to play at. If you want to play the clip at half speed enter 50%. If you want the shot to play at double speed enter 200%.

4 The duration of the shot in the Timeline will now change according to the value entered. Depending on which Mac you are using the shot may now have to be rendered for playback. If there is a red line above the shot this indicates the shot must be rendered. Other colors indicate some level of playback will be possible.

01:00:02:00 01:00:04:00 01:00

ddah Impressiv Candles 2 (50%) Face in the s

5 Select the Sequence menu at the top of your screen and scroll down to Render Video. Check that there is a tick next to the color which corresponds with the colored line above the shot in your sequence. For example, if there is a red line you will need a tick next to the red Needs Render setting. Likewise, if there is a green line, check there is a tick next to the green Preview. These settings toggle on and off.

Both
Video
✓ — Needs Render
— Rendered Proxy
Proxy
✓ — Preview
— Full
✓ — Unlimited
Audio ⌃·
✓ — For Playback

Sequence Effects Tools Window Help

Render ▶ Both ⌘R
Render All ▶ Video
✓ — Needs Render
— Rendered Proxy
Proxy
✓ — Preview

6 Select Render Video from the Sequence menu. Once your effect has been rendered you can play back the result.

103

To play a clip in reverse simply check the 'reverse' option in the speed dialog box or enter a negative value.

It is worth noting that you may be able to play back the result without rendering by using the RT Extreme facility within Final Cut Pro. For a true

Constant Speed ‡
Duration: 00:00:02:20
Speed: 50 percent
☑ Reverse
☑ Frame Blending

representation of the final result it is best to render the clip. This will give you full resolution playback.

Split Edits

In most situations where an edit takes place both video and audio will cut at the same point. This is fine for most situations. However, in other situations a technique known as a Split Edit may be used. A Split Edit is where audio and video do not cut at exactly the same place – either one may precede the other and this can apply to either the 'in' or 'out' point of an edit – thus audio or video may start and/or finish at separate points.

Split Editing is a technique often used in news and documentaries, particularly in interview situations. For example, you may hear a person speaking over visuals of a scene being described. After several seconds, with the voice of the person still running, the video will cut to the person speaking.

To achieve a Split Edit:

1   Open a shot into the Viewer.

2   Position the Scrubber Bar where you wish to mark the edit.

3   Hold down the Control key and click in the white area in the Viewer (where you mark 'in' and 'out' points). This will open the contextual menu which is used for

clearing and setting 'in' and 'out' points. At the bottom of this menu is an option for Mark Split.

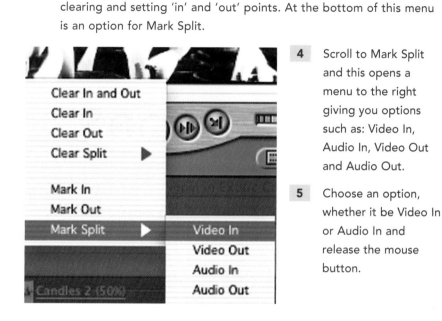

4   Scroll to Mark Split and this opens a menu to the right giving you options such as: Video In, Audio In, Video Out and Audio Out.

5   Choose an option, whether it be Video In or Audio In and release the mouse button.

6   Reposition the Scrubber Bar and now choose the opposite choice – if you have already marked Video In, now choose Audio In.

7   Repeat the process for the end of the edit. You can mark separate video and audio 'out' points. If you do not want separate video and audio 'out' points then mark an 'out' point by simply pressing 'o'.

8   Position the Scrubber Bar in the Timeline and use Overwrite to edit the shot into the Timeline.

Play back the edit and watch the result. If you have followed all of the above steps the audio and video will cut in the Timeline at separate places. If you marked a split for the end point audio and video will finish at separate places.

Achieving Split Edits in Final Cut Pro is not the easiest of functions but it is definitely worth learning. Once mastered you can add finesse to a film and boost it into the professional realm. Any editor worth their salt will understand the process of performing Split Edits and know how and where to use them.

The Split Edit is also reflected visually in the Timeline. If you look at your audio and video tracks you will be able to see where the audio and video edits take place. If it is not clear you may have to use the Magnifier tool to increase the size of the Timeline and then each of the edits will be more obvious.

If you find the above process difficult to follow there is another way to achieve Split Edits. This is done by Locking Tracks and editing directly in the Timeline with the Razorblade.

1 Lock the tracks you do not wish to affect, for example lock your two audio tracks.

2 Select the Razorblade tool from the Toolbar.

3 Cut the video at the point where you want the Split Edit to occur.

4 Choose the Pointer tool and highlight the piece of video you wish to remove. Press the Delete key.

5 Drag the end of the shot to fill the gap created when the razorbladed section was deleted.

You may find that it is not possible to drag the end of the shot to fill the gap. This could be because you are at the end of the media limit. All non-linear editing systems work by referencing to the original media stored on hard disk. If all the media of a particular clip is already edited into the Timeline then it will be impossible to extract more frames.

Another way to achieve Split Edits is to use the break-off tabs in the Timeline and to restrict the flow of video or audio. For example, if the break-off tabs for Audio 1 and Audio 2 are disconnected then only the video will flow through when performing an Overwrite Edit. Using the break-off tabs is like turning a tap on or off. If it's connected it is open – if it's disconnected it is closed.

Drag and Drop Editing

The editing we have done so far has involved opening a clip in the Viewer, marking an 'in' and 'out' point, and then editing this clip into the Timeline via the Canvas. It is possible to bypass this method altogether and edit clips directly from the Browser into the Timeline, or to edit from the Viewer to the Timeline without involving the Canvas in the equation.

1   Create a New Sequence in the Browser (press Apple N).

2   Double click the new Sequence to open it – you can rename the Sequence if you wish.

3   In the Browser click once on any of the clips – do not release the mouse button (open a bin if all your clips are filed away).

4   With the mouse button still depressed drag the clip from the Browser directly into the Timeline. Release the mouse button and your clip will be edited into the Timeline at the position where you released your mouse button.

5   Do this again with a few more clips and you will see that it is possible to build a sequence simply by dragging clips from the Browser to the Timeline.

6   Once you have several clips positioned in the Timeline repeat the procedure, however, this time drag the clip into the middle of the Timeline. Don't release your mouse button just yet!

When you have your clip positioned in the Timeline move the mouse button gently and notice that if you have the cursor pointing to the top third of the video track there is a horizontal arrow – if you point the cursor toward the bottom half of the screen there is a vertical arrow. A horizontal arrow represents Insert Edit while a vertical arrow represents Overwrite Edit.

Drag Clip to Bottom of Video Track – Overwrite Edit

Drag Clip to Top of Video Track – Insert Edit

The biggest disadvantage with using Drag and Drop editing is that you do not have the control over marking the 'in' and 'out' points of the clip in the Viewer. However, this can be a very quick way to throw clips together into the Timeline. Furthermore, you can also do two other very useful tricks using Drag and Drop.

First, if you work in picture icon view you can arrange the icons in whichever order you choose (arrange them left to right in storyboard fashion) and then, by selecting an entire group of clips (by lassoing, or by

using Alt and clicking to select multiple clips) you can then drag as many items as you wish into the Timeline. These clips will be positioned in the Timeline in order of the icon arrangement.

Buddah Impressive	Candles 3	Elephant
dah Impressive	Candles 3	Elephant
dah Impressive	Candles 3	Elephant

Once the clips have been dropped into the Timeline the Razorblade can be used to chop away unwanted sections. If you really wanted, you could edit in this way without ever opening a clip in the Viewer or dragging across to the Canvas (however, I would never rely on this exclusively as my method of editing).

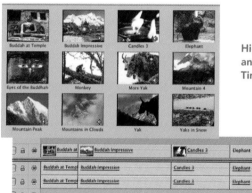

Highlight the Icons in the Browser and Drag these Directly into the Timeline

The Clips will then be Arranged in the Timeline in the Order they were Positioned in the Browser

It is also worth noting that it is possible to drag clips from the Viewer to the Timeline, thus skipping out the step of editing across to the Canvas. The same rules apply when dragging clips from the Browser to the Timeline. If you have a horizontal arrow this will represent an Insert Edit, while if you have a vertical arrow an Overwrite Edit will occur. You can also mark 'in' and 'out' points in the Viewer in the usual way. These 'in' and 'out' points will apply and therefore determine the beginning and end of the edit.

If clips are not open in the Viewer the 'in' and 'out' points will still apply. Thus should you drag a clip directly from the Browser into the Timeline, the duration of the edit and the start/end frame of the clip will be defined by the 'in' and 'out' points which have previously been set.

Extending/Reducing Clips by Dragging

Clips can be made longer or shorter by grabbing hold of either end and dragging the length in either direction.

1   Choose a clip in the Timeline which you wish to extend or reduce. Position the pointer and let it hover over the center of an edit point or the area where two clips meet. A symbol with two vertical lines and two horizontal arrows will appear.

2   If you wish to reduce the length of the clip drag the end of the clip into itself (using the symbol with two vertical lines). A display will appear to the right showing the overall clip duration and the trim adjustment in seconds and frames.

At the same time the Canvas will shuttle through the clip as you drag the end, giving you a visual reference to the adjustments being made. You therefore have a display in both the Timeline and the Canvas giving you numeric and visual indicators at the same time.

Providing you have Linked Selection switched on audio and video will move together, otherwise they will be independent.

3   In order to extend the length of a clip a gap must exist between the clip you wish to extend and the clip adjacent to it. To create a gap

either insert a shot and then delete it and a gap will be created, or use the Arrow tool to highlight and drag several clips further along the Timeline.

Create a Gap

Extend the Length of the Clip into the
Gap you have Created

If you find it impossible to extend the length of a clip it most likely means there is no more material left to extract from the original clip. All clips have a media limit as defined by the amount of material originally captured to hard drive. Once this media limit is reached you can go no further.

For fine control when dragging, hold down the Alt/Option key. Another way to achieve fine control is to expand the Timeline by using either the Magnifier tool or the Slider Bar at the bottom of the Timeline.

RENDERING

It is a unique editor. And there's nothing like it out there.
CHARLES ROBERTS
MEDIA PROFESSOR, AUTHOR, EDITOR

Rendering is the process by which your computer builds each of the individual frames needed to produce an effect. When you play back straight cuts in the Timeline nothing needs to be rendered. The computer simply refers to the hard drive where the original shot has been recorded and uses your edit information to determine which section of the original shot is needed. When an effect is applied to a clip a different process must take place.

People often complain about rendering – to wait seconds or minutes for a computer to produce an effect can often drive people mad. I always smile at these situations. My background was in the world of on-line tape editing where the editor would work with several videotape machines, a separate vision mixer, character generator, audio mixer and Digital Video Effects (DVE) generator. To produce effects in this setup would often require an editor to record one or more of the shots to separate tapes. Several tape machines would then be run in sync with the layered effects built through the mix-effects banks of a vision mixer. The output would be in real time, however, real time was only achieved at the expense of the time used in the setup of an effect. These effects would often take a considerable amount of time to set up.

It is not always necessary to render effects in Final Cut Pro to see a result. Through the facility known as RT Extreme it is possible to see many effects play back in real time directly through Firewire. One should be aware, however, that the output quality is not always full quality and that the results are intended for the purpose of gauging timing and other critical decisions, rather than for producing full resolution output. The final output will still need to be rendered. The advantage of RT Extreme is that it allows the editor, in many situations, to build effects without having the render process getting in the way of one's creative flow.

Dynamic RT is a mode in RT Extreme which allows the computer to automatically adjust image quality and frame-rate on-the-fly so you always get the best possible real-time playback on your system. So if an effect is complex the frame-rate and image quality will drop, so you can see the result with lesser quality. A simpler effect will playback at full frame-rate and higher quality.

The amount of real time one gets through RT Extreme and Dynamic RT depends on the processor inside your Mac, which Mac you are using, the amount of installed memory, the system bus speed of the computer, how many layers, filters, transitions and generators are being used and the complexity of the effects created.

A further factor to consider is the setting chosen in the Real-time Effects pop-up menu. The output quality for RT Extreme is customizable. You choose the quality you want the output to be played back at.

Unlimited RT allows Final Cut Pro to play the maximum possible in the way of real-time effects; however, the trade-off is an increased likelihood of dropped frames. Choosing **Safe RT** will eliminate dropped frames, however, this will limit the overall ability to playback effects in real time.

My choice is to leave Unlimited RT set. I can live with dropped frames. If I need full quality results then I render.

I leave **Dynamic RT** switched on for both Playback Video Quality and Playback Frame Rate. This means the computer will vary the output quality according to the complexity of the effects.

Leave Record to Tape on Full Quality as this will give you full resolution output when recording.

Multiclip Playback is relevant to Multicam (dealt with later). I always leave this switched on.

Don't stress out about your RT Extreme and Dynamic RT settings. You set these according to your choice and then forget about them.

The Render Settings

In the early versions of Final Cut Pro the render settings were basic. One could choose to render everything in the Timeline or one could choose to render a particular section. Now the choices are far greater. The choices give power to the editor. One can be quite specific about which sections of the Timeline one wishes to render.

Sequence	Effects	Tools	Window	Help	
Render			▶	**Both**	⌘R
Render All			▶	**Video**	
Render Only			▶	✓ ▬ **Needs Render**	
Settings...			⌘0	▬ **Rendered Proxy**	
				Proxy	
Lift			⌫	✓ ▬ **Preview**	
Ripple Delete			⇧⌫	▬ **Full**	
Close Gap			^G	✓ ▬ **Unlimited**	
Solo Selected Item(s)			^S	**Audio**	^⌥R
Nest Item(s)...			⌥C	✓ ▬ **For Playback**	
Add Edit			^V	▬ **Item Level**	

1 Choose the Sequence menu and scroll to Render – a window opens displaying various colors. These are the options one can choose when setting the level to which you want the Render command to apply.

2 You can choose as many or as few of the colors to apply to this setting as you wish. Each level, represented by a color, works by means of a toggle. A tick means a color is selected; no tick means it is not selected. You need to choose the colors you want to apply to the Render Selection setting. This is achieved by clicking on a setting and releasing your mouse button. The color that you clicked will now have a tick next to it. Each time you wish to activate or deactivate a particular setting you need to repeat the process.

3 Do the same for the Render All settings under the Sequence menu and the Render Only setting. Render All applies to the entire Timeline, whereas Render Only applies to a particular color, or level of render,

Sequence	Effects	Tools	Window	Help

Render	▶
Render All	▶
Render Only	▶
Settings...	⌘0
Lift	⌫

Both ↰

Video

✓ ━ Needs Render
✓ ━ Rendered Proxy
✓   Proxy
✓ ━ Preview
✓ ━ Full
✓ ━ Unlimited

Audio

✓ ━ For Playback
    ━ Item Level

throughout the Timeline. Once the settings have been chosen these settings will be remembered by Final Cut Pro each time you open the program.

At a basic level, one could select the color red. When a red bar is exhibited above a clip, it means the real-time capabilities of Final Cut Pro have been exceeded and the material must then be rendered for playback.

Sequence 25	Wild Creatures	Great Shots

1:00:12:00   01:00:18:00   01:00

The following is a basic summary of what the most important of the individual colors mean:

Dark Gray – no rendering is required.

Steel Gray – material in the Timeline has been rendered.

Dark Green – will play back through RT Extreme at full quality.

Green – will play back through RT Extreme, however, motion and scaling effects will be approximate only.

Yellow – will play back through RT Extreme with an approximate representation of the effect. Some filter controls may be ignored.

Orange – effects will be played back with a high likelihood of dropped frames.

Red – requires rendering for playback.

The render commands I use most are to Render a particular part of the Timeline – accessed by holding down the Apple key and the letter 'R', or Render All, accessed by holding down the Alt/Option key and pressing 'R'. This will render all the video in the Timeline that requires rendering. By accessing the Sequence menu the commands can also be executed. One can choose to render Both – which means Video and Audio, or Video or Audio Independently.

Apple + R – Render highlighted video in the Timeline
Alt/Option + R – Render all video in the Timeline

You need to configure the render options to suit your needs. My choice is to keep life really simple. I select all the options possible. This means I know that everything necessary for a full quality render will be performed when I hit any of the render commands.

Whenever you see a red bar at the top of the Timeline (above a shot to which an effect has been applied) this means this section must be rendered. It is possible to render individual clips or to instruct the computer to render everything in the Timeline that needs rendering.

When a shot requires rendering, go to the Sequence menu at the top of your screen and scroll down to Render. Providing you have the appropriate colors selected to match the color of what needs to be rendered, the process will then begin.

A progress bar will display in percentage terms how much material has been rendered.

Once the render is complete you can then play the rendered clip/s in real time. If you are happy with the result, carry on editing. If you are not happy make the necessary adjustments to the parameters of the effect and then render again.

At any time you can stop a render in mid-progress by pressing the Escape key (located top left of your keyboard). The render will cease, however, the portion of the shot or Sequence already rendered can be played back. This is a particularly useful feature as one can choose to render a small portion of a shot or Sequence, then play back this section to determine whether or not to go ahead with the complete render. Once you restart the render process begins again at the point where it was previously stopped. Thus, you do not need to re-render material that has already been rendered just because you stopped the process mid-render to look at the result of an effect.

A final useful work tip. If you mark the 'in' and 'out' points in the Timeline, you can then choose the Render Selection command found under the Sequence menu. This will render everything between the 'in' and the 'out' points. Very useful!

Sequence	Effects	Tools
Render Selection		

Sequence	Effects	Tools	Window	Help
Render ▶	Both	⌘R		
Render All ▶	Video			
Render Only ▶	✓ ▬ Needs Render			
	✓ ▬ Rendered Proxy			
	✓ Proxy			
	✓ ▬ Preview			
	✓ ▬ Full			
	✓ ▬ Unlimited			
	Audio	^⌥R		
	✓ ▬ For Playback			
	✓ ▬ Item Level			

One can choose to be selective about what gets rendered in the Timeline, or simply switch on all the render controls and this will ensure that everything that needs rendering will be rendered when the command is given.

Open Format Timeline

One of the new features in Final Cut Pro 6 is the ability to edit mixed formats into the Final Cut Pro Timeline and to be able to play back the different formats in real time without having to render until final output.

It used to be when one set up their Timeline in Easy Setup everything would work for the format which was specified. Choose DV-PAL and you cut DV-PAL, but introduce some DVCPro HD and some DVCPro 50 footage and suddenly the render bars would appear. This interrupts the creative flow as the editor hits Apple + R and then waits until the render process is done.

That's how it used to be.

With Mixed Format editing you get a lot more. Many formats at different frame rates play together in real time. While there can still be some render bars which appear, depending on the complexity of the codecs at work and the power of your Mac, for the most one can cut from one format to another with a lot less pain than in previous versions of Final Cut Pro. A final render is still needed for final output. While editing, for the most, the different formats play together in real time.

The mixed format Timeline on the previous page shows most formats will play in real time. Final Cut does have some difficulty playing back in real time H.264, however this is designed as a distribution format and not as an editing format, so this is to be expected. Note the XDCam 1080p24 gave a red bar for rendering the audio and not the video. The test machine was a MacBook Pro with Intel dual core duo 2.33 GHz and 2 GB ram. The Timeline was set to DVCPro HD 1080i50.

It is important to be aware of how the Open Format Timeline handles scaling.

Go to User Preferences and look to the second tab at the top titled Editing.

General | Editing | Labels | Timeline Options | Render Control | Audio Outputs

ce ▲▼

☑ Always Reconnect Externally Modified Files
☑ Warn on "Send to Soundtrack Pro Script"

Jon-Drop ▲▼

Auto conform sequence: Ask ▲▼

☑ Always scale clips to sequence size

Cancel   OK

To the bottom right is an option to scale your clip in size according to the Sequence Settings of your Timeline. This can be toggled on off.

When leaving this option on it means that SD footage in a HD timeline will be scaled larger to fill the HD frame – or vice versa, scaled down in size if HD footage is edited into a SD Timeline.

4:3 SD to HD: Scaling On

4:3 SD to HD: Scaling Off

MEDIA
MANAGEMENT

You have high-end, professional, 'broadcast and beyond'
capable tools in an easy to use package that anybody can learn.
JIM KANTER
ATLANTA FINAL CUT PRO USER GROUP

In an ideal world when one completes a project it should be as simple as deleting the files from the scratch disks which were chosen during initial setup. In reality, editors will often end up with files scattered across several hard disks with everything from clips to render files in the most obscure and hidden areas of one's computer. This situation is particularly common when one works with several projects at a time and when one fails to pay attention to the setup of scratch disks when moving from project to project. Fortunately there are a few very easy techniques which one can use without having to search through every folder on each hard drive to track down all of the files that have been used in a particular project.

Making Clips Offline

An invaluable command is **Make Offline** found under the Modify menu. Make Offline, as the name suggests, will break the link between the project you are working with and the clips you choose to make offline. This is done in one of three ways:

(1) the link is broken and the clips are left stored on the hard drive

(2) the selected clips are moved to the trash

(3) the selected clips are deleted from the disk.

1 Highlight the items in the Browser which you wish to Make Offline. Clips, bins or Sequences can be chosen.

2 Select the Modify menu and scroll to Make Offline. A box will open giving you three options.

3 Choose the option you wish to perform.

▶ 🗀 Extras
▼ 🗀 Great Shots
  🎞 Buddah at Temple
  🎞 Buddah Impressive
  🎞 Candles 3
  🎞 Elephant

After making selected clips offline...

┌ **Action For Media Files:** ──────

  ⦿ **Leave Them on the Disk**
  ◯ **Move Them to the Trash**
  ◯ **Delete Them from the Disk**

You can choose to make the clips offline and leave them stored on the hard drive where they already exist, or move them to the trash, or delete them from disk. If you choose either of the last two options be careful as the results cannot be undone.

I often use Make Offline and select Delete Them from the Disk at the end of a project. This ensures a quick easy way to clear the captured media files from the hard drives in your computer with the minimum of effort on your part.

It can also be useful to move a bunch of files, or all the files of a project, to the trash, to copy elsewhere. This is the simplest way of tracking down all the files in a project without having to manually search for them.

The Render Manager

Whenever you render material in the Timeline the files created during the render process are stored in the Render folder/s created when you set your scratch disks. Due to the nature of building effects material will often be rendered several times over until you get the effect exactly as you want it. It can therefore be advantageous to get rid of old render files which are not being used anymore and reclaim the hard drive space. This is exactly what the Render Manager does for you – it clears out the render files you no longer need in a simple and efficient way.

1   Choose the Tools menu, scroll to Render Manager and release your mouse button. A window will open displaying folders which reference to the render files on your hard drives.

2   Click the downward arrows to reveal the render files. Information to the right will tell you the amount of hard drive space these files take up.

Tools	Window	Help
Audio Mixer		
Frame Viewer		
QuickView		
Video Scopes		
Voice Over		
Button Bars		
Button List		
Control Surfaces...		
FXBuilder		
Keyboard Layout		
Render Manager...		

Name	Type	Size	Remove
▼ 📁 Additional Render Files	Bin	88.3 MB	
▼ 📁 FCP4 Cover Pict.	Bin	41.2 MB	
▼ 📁 Graham Cutout	Bin	41.2 MB	
🖼 Video	Render Files	41.2 MB	
▼ 📁 Final Cut Express Cover copy	Bin	5.9 MB	
▼ 📁 Sequence 1	Bin	5.9 MB	
🖼 Video	Render Files	5.9 MB	
▼ 📁 Footage Library	Bin	41.2 MB	
▶ 📁 Sequence 3	Bin	41.2 MB	
▼ 📁 Billy Story Cover	Bin	56.6 MB	
▼ 📁 Sequence 2	Bin	56.6 MB	

3   Highlight the files you wish to remove. Apple click to highlight multiple files, one at a time, or Shift click to highlight everything from top to bottom.

Name	Type	Size
▼ 📁 Additional Render Files	Bin	88.3 M
▼ 📁 FCP4 Cover Pict.	Bin	41.2 M
▼ 📁 Graham Cutout	Bin	41.2 M
📹 Video	Render Files	41.2 M
▶ 📁 Final Cut Express Cover copy	Bin	5.9 MB
▶ 📁 Footage Library	Bin	41.2 M
▼ 📁 Billy Story Cover	Bin	56.6 M
▼ 📁 Sequence 2	Bin	56.6 M
📹 Video	Render Files	56.6 M

4 Click OK and these files will be deleted from the disk.

Note: the results cannot be undone as the files have now been removed from disk, however, you can simply re-render the material if you find you have made a mistake. Nothing will be lost but the time it takes to render.

EFFECTS

When working with Transitions and Filters these are applied to a single layer of video and can be integrated into a Sequence which is made up of no more than a single video track. This does not mean that Sequences made up of multiple layers do not use Transitions and Filters. The point is a Sequence made up of no more than one layer can include Transitions, Filters and Generators. Multi-layered Sequences will also make use of Transitions, Filters and Generators and these can and likely will be applied to any of the layers in the Sequence.

The instant you have more than one layer of video you are working in the realms of compositing. Layers are video components which are stacked on top of each other – examples include: picture in picture, titles, and animated components.

An Example of Compositing Made Up of Two Video Layers

An Example of Compositing Made Up of Three Video Layers

Before we move onto Compositing it is important to know how to work with Transitions, Filters and Generators. You need to understand the difference between these. Just to refresh your memory: Transitions work between clips; Filters are applied to clips; and Generators work in a similar way to clips but are generated within Final Cut Pro itself.

The Concept of Media Limit (Handles)

It is vital to understand when using Transitions that there must be available media for the Transition to work. This available media is referred to as 'handles'. The maximum length that a Transition can be is equal to the available media or 'handles' which exist on the original clips as they were captured to your computer's hard drive.

Thus, should you wish to apply a one second dissolve between two shots then there must be at least 12 frames (PAL) or 15 frames (NTSC) of available media. The available media applies to the end (tail) of the outgoing clip, on one side of the transition, and the beginning or 'head' of the incoming clip. The idea is the same as checkerboarding two pieces of film in an optical printer or A/B rolling shots on separate machines in a linear tape suite.

If you do not have the available media then the length of a transition will be restricted to the media that is available. It is impossible to exceed these limits.

Applying Transitions

1   Click once on the Effects tab in the Browser and this will reveal a list of Transitions, Filters and Generators. I suggest working in list mode for this part of the operation.

2   Click once on the triangle to the left of the Video Transitions folder – this will reveal a list of the available Transitions. Choose the type of transition you require and click the triangle to the left. Now choose a transition you want to work with.

3   Drag the Transition onto the edit point in the Timeline where you want the effect to be applied.

4   A render bar will appear indicating the state of the material in the Timeline. If it is red, it needs to be rendered for playback, if it is green the effect will play in real time through RT Extreme. If it is yellow or orange the effect will play, however, the reliability of playback cannot be guaranteed.

Note: when choosing Transitions, Filters or Generators if the effect is bold under the Effects tab in the Browser, this means the effect will play in real time through RT Extreme. If the effect is not in bold then it will have to be rendered for playback.

Changing Transition Durations

1   Double click on the Transition in the Timeline – this will open a set of controls in the Viewer.

2 At the top of the Viewer is the name of the Transition. Immediately below this is a numerical value representing the Transition duration. Click once with the mouse in this box and this will highlight the numeric value. You can now overtype this value. If you want a 2 second dissolve type 200 and press the return button; if you want a half second dissolve type 12 (PAL) or 15 (NTSC) and press return; for a 10 second dissolve type 1000 and press the return button.

The Change in Transition Duration is Reflected in the Timeline

3 The dissolve duration is now changed. The above set of instructions applies regardless of which transition is chosen.

Applying Filters

Filters are extremely powerful and creative tools to work with. It can take a good deal of experimentation to master them. It is definitely worth the effort, however. What can be produced on a desktop editing system such as Final Cut Pro would have cost a fortune at a facilities house only a few years ago. The price paid now is the amount of time the individual is prepared to spend building and rendering these effects.

1 Click on the triangle to the left of Video Filters in the effects area of the Browser. This will reveal a list of Filters stored in bins. Open a bin and choose a Filter you wish to experiment with.

2   Drag the Filter onto the clip where you want the Filter to be applied.
    Remember, if the Filter is bold this indicates it will play in real time
    through RT Extreme. If it is not bold it will need to be rendered. The
    level of real-time playback will be determined by the color of the render
    bar which appears above the clip in the Timeline.

3   To alter the parameters of the Filter double click the clip in the Timeline.
    Click on the Filters tab located at the top of the Viewer.

This will open a selection of controls that are used to alter the
parameters of the filter.

4 Make sure the Scrubber
Bar in the Timeline is
positioned on the clip to
which the Filter has been
applied. This is important
as it ensures adjustments
will be displayed visually
in the Canvas.

5 Experiment with the controls under the Filters tab in the Viewer and
observe the result in the Canvas and on your television screen (if you
are set up with this configuration). Play the clip back through
RT Extreme, if possible, or render the clip if necessary.

All Transitions and Filters can also be accessed from the Effects menu at the top of the screen. Simply scroll down to Video Transitions or Video Filters and select the effect you want. If you wish to use a Transition make sure the Scrubber Bar in the Timeline is positioned where the Transition is to be applied. If you choose a Filter, first highlight the clip in the Timeline and then choose the Filter from the Effects menu. Whether you choose to access the effects from the Effects menu or from the Effects tab in the Browser comes down to personal preference. The result will be the same.

Compositing

Compositing is where all the fancy stuff happens: flying titles, moving boxes, multi-layered dissolve sequences, transparent backgrounds – all the elements that 'dress up' a video production and make it more than cuts, dissolves, basic transitions and filters. As mentioned earlier, compositing encompasses everything that involves more than one layer of video.

Video filters, transitions and generators can all be applied to any video track, or several individual video tracks at a time, however, it is the 'stacking' or 'layering' of tracks of video that builds a composited sequence.

In on-line linear suites layering of video was done on a vision mixer in combination with a DVE (digital video effects). In the film world an optical printer was used.

Pieces of film were sandwiched together (called bi-packing) and this was then exposed to several passes of light to achieve complex effects. Inside of Final Cut Pro the tracks are layered in hierarchical order with the tracks closest to the top having priority over those below.

For those who have no idea what a DVE is – this refers to a stand-alone box used in television production for creating special effects. DVEs became popular in the late 1970s and 1980s and have been used all the way through to the present. DVEs have been seen as providing the video equivalent to the optical printer of the film world. They have traditionally been regarded as horrendously expensive, powerful devices. They are still used in live television production and on-line edit suites, however, as a result of programs such as Final Cut Pro mere mortals can now achieve sophisticated effects with modest budgets. Previously a simple squeeze or flip (or flop as it is called in Final Cut Pro) required one to step into an expensive post-production suite and often pay far more than the cost of Final Cut Pro for a single effect!

Methods of Creating Multiple Tracks

By default Final Cut Pro opens with a single track of video in the Timeline. There are three possible ways to add more tracks:

(i) Control click next to the V1, V2 symbols (to the left of the locks). This will give you the option to either Add or Delete a track. If you click in

the gray area above the last existing video track there will be a single option which is to add a track.

(ii) Drag a clip from the Browser or Viewer directly into the Timeline, into the gray area, above the top-most existing video track. Release

your mouse button. This will then create a new video track where you drop the clip and two audio tracks below the last existing audio tracks.

(iii) Open the Sequence menu at the top of screen and choose the Insert Tracks command from the menu.

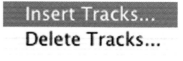

Once you have created the additional video tracks, items can then be edited to these tracks by dragging clips from the Browser or Viewer directly into the Timeline, or you can direct the flow of video/audio using the break-off tab patching facility in combination with Insert and Overwrite Editing.

The Motion Tab

The Motion tab is home to a great many of the tools used in the compositing process. In this window you will find the facility to resize images, rotate, reposition, crop, distort and adjust the opacity of clips. Effectively the Motion tab provides you, the editor, with a fully fledged DVE facility.

To access the Motion tab, click the last tab to the right in the Viewer. Click the arrows to the left of each of the headings to access the controls.

Using the Motion Tab

To **scale** an image means to reduce or increase its size. The default size is 100%, therefore numbers greater than 100 mean the image has been made larger or 'blown' up whereas numbers less than 100 mean the image has been reduced in size.

To alter the size of a clip using the Motion tab:

1 Double click a clip in the Timeline. This will open the clip into the Viewer. Make sure the yellow Scrubber Bar is positioned on the clip in the Timeline. This ensures you will see the result in the Canvas as you alter the parameters of the clip in the Motion tab.

2 Click the Motion tab in the Viewer.

3 Move the slider bar next to the word Scale either backwards or forwards. Alternatively type in a number. If you wish to reduce the clip in size by half type 50%. If you want to double its size type 200%.

Providing the clip is positioned on video 1 in the Timeline the result will be the image, reduced in size, over black. If you do not see this result you need to position the yellow Scrubber Bar over the clip in the Timeline prior to reducing the image in size.

Now repeat the process, however, this time we want to work with two tracks of video.

1 Create a second track of video by Control clicking in the gray area above V1.

2   Select Add Track.

3   Slide the V1 break-off tab to V2 and edit a clip onto V2. Alternatively, you can drag a clip direct from the Browser or Viewer to V2.

4   Reduce the size of an image on the V2 track to 50%. This will create what is called a 'picture in picture'. The image on the V2 track will be reduced in size while that on V1 remains at 100%.

Providing your computer is capable of RT Extreme, and External Video is set to All Frames and the Firewire cable is connected to a deck/camera, then you will be able to see the result play in real time onto a television monitor. If you are working exclusively on the computer monitor and not connected to a deck/camera then you can observe the result in the Canvas.

To rotate the image on the V2 track simply select the rotate command underneath Scale.

Turn the wheel or type in a numeric value.

Remember – a circle is made up of 360 degrees.

Again, to ensure the clip is active in the Viewer, first double click it in the Timeline. Then click the Motion tab to see the controls, making sure the yellow

Scrubber Bar is positioned on the clip in the Timeline/ Canvas. This will ensure the result is displayed in the Canvas.

To move a clip about within the Canvas click on the plus '+' symbol to the right of the word Center in the motion controls. A small '+' will then appear in the Canvas (you might have to look hard to see it – but it is there!) Click the '+' with your mouse and reposition the image within the Canvas window. Alternatively, type co-ordinates into the boxes.

As you work, you may choose to rotate the image again or resize it. Other parameters can be altered. For example, check the Drop Shadow box towards the bottom of the Motion window.

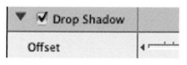

Experimentation is the key. By adjusting parameters, typing numbers, adjusting opacity, altering angles – many different results can be achieved. No instruction manual can ever teach you everything that is possible. It is up to you to teach yourself by altering the controls and trying out the possibilities.

Image + Wireframe

An important and useful mode is what is called Image + Wireframe. Click the arrow in the box located towards the center of the Canvas. Select Image + Wireframe from the drop-down menu.

Once you have selected Image + Wireframe you will notice a large cross will appear from end to end across

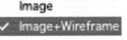

the active image. When working in this mode it is possible to slide the

Click on Center of the Image and Reposition by Dragging

image around the frame by simply clicking on the center of the image with your cursor and then repositioning by dragging. This is a lot simpler than typing in center co-ordinates into the boxes or using the little '+' symbol as described earlier.

Below: The image can be rotated by positioning your cursor on either edge and moving your mouse in opposite directions.

Your Cursor Becomes a
Circular Arrow. You can
then Rotate the Image

Below: By dragging any of the corners of the image it can quickly be resized.

Position Your Cursor on
the Edge of the Image and
Drag to Resize

Using Image + Wireframe provides a quick and effective way to reposition, resize and rotate images. The downside is you do not get the same control which you do by entering numerical values directly into the Motion Control window. Choose whichever option suits the task you need to perform.

Titlesafe

Under the same menu as Image + Wireframe is another setting called Titlesafe. Both settings, Image + Wireframe and Titlesafe, can be switched on or off in either the Viewer or Canvas.

If you find it impossible to switch on Titlesafe you need to first ensure that Show Overlays is checked. With Show Overlays selected it is then possible to toggle Titlesafe on and off.

The Titlesafe setting is particularly important to have switched on when positioning images or working with titles. Domestic monitors do not display the full video image as it is recorded to tape. What is displayed on your computer monitor known as 'underscan' while what you see on your television set is known as 'overscan'. Broadcast monitors offer both options.

When Titlesafe is switched on it will be obvious – two sets of blue lines will be noticeable around the inside perimeter of the Viewer or Canvas. The Title Safe area is known as the Essential Message Area (EMA). In simple terms, to ensure that the images you are working with will be seen correctly on a television set you need to make sure they are positioned within the lines of the Title Safe area. The outer lines are regarded as safe on most televisions, whereas the inner lines are regarded as safe on virtually all television sets. When working with text it is best to position the text inside the inner lines. When positioning images do not go outside of the outer lines unless you are comfortable that these images will likely spill outside the frame, or cut-off, on playback. Of course, allowing images to spill outside of cut-off can be used for effect, however, one needs to know that this will take place. In other words, if this effect takes place it should be deliberate, rather than accidental.

It is important to remember that not all television sets are the same. Some will crop the final images on playback more than others.

Working with Multi-Layers

It is relatively easy to create a picture in picture as already described. Using the same principles one can position several images on-screen at a time. The effect we will produce is to have a single image positioned as a background with three other images layered over it. Prior to the availability of systems such as Final Cut Pro this type of effect could only be produced at facility companies and television stations using powerful DVEs and other expensive equipment. Now you can do it on your desktop quickly and easily.

1   Layer the images you want to work with over each other in the Timeline. Be aware that the order in which they are stacked will determine the priority of the layers.

Thus the image on layer 4 will be at the front of the layers, while the image in layer 1 will serve as the background. Those on V2 and V3 will make up the middle layers.

2   Reduce each of the images in size to 35% – except for the background image, this stays at 100%. To achieve this you will need to individually click on each of the images to bring them into the Viewer, and then resize accordingly. To achieve the same size for each image make sure the number in the Scale setting is the same.

3   Make sure that Image + Wireframe is switched on and use your mouse to position each of the images. You will need to double click each clip in the Timeline to make it active in the Viewer, then position accordingly. Repeat this procedure for each image you wish to position. This can be done manually or, if you prefer, use the '+' symbol to set X and Y co-ordinates in the Motion Control window.

4   If you find there is a black border on any of the edges as you place the images, you need to use the Crop facility to remove this. Often a black edge is seen on the extreme outer perimeter of the video frame. This is never seen when the image is played to a television set, however, when an image is squeezed back this can become apparent. It needs to be cropped to get rid of it.

Use the slider bars to crop the image or enter a numeric value to achieve the same result.

5 Switch on the Drop Shadow in the Motion Control window. Controls for this setting are used to indicate the direction, distance, color, softness and opacity of the drop shadow.		▼ ☑ Drop Shadow
		Offset
		Angle
		Color
		Softness

If necessary, reduce the opacity of the bottom layer to make the images on the upper layers stand out. This is achieved by using the opacity slider in the Motion window or by switching on Clip Overlays at the base of the Timeline and then moving the bar which appears within the clip to the desired level. A counter will indicate shifts in the level of opacity as you move the bar up and down.

The Slider Bar Affects the Opacity of Clips

Clip Overlays

Move the Black Bar Up and Down to Adjust Opacity

It is best to plan your effects before you begin to create them. By having a clear picture of what you are trying to achieve you have a much better chance of achieving something that works. By all means experiment. It is better, however, to experiment with vision and purpose rather than stumbling around in the dark hoping something acceptable will emerge.

Keyframing Images

Keyframing allows you to set points which define a path which an effect will follow. It provides the ability to move things around, animate objects in real time and perform subtle or fast moves. An example of keyframing would be to move a box from one side of the screen to another. Effects are built through layering and adjustments to the attributes in the Motion Control tab such as size, rotation and position.

To keyframe an image you must first decide what you are trying to achieve. Let us work through the following example where we will have an image start on one side of the screen, rotate gently and increase in size until it comes to rest on the other side of the screen.

Two layers of video are involved with this example.

Layer 1 – Mountains
Layer 2 – Balloon

When keyframing images I change the layout of the interface. You may wish to learn this as a custom setup so that you can quickly move back and forth between the standard setup and the setup used for compositing and motion control.

The Motion tab is positioned on top of the Browser and extended to reveal its full width. Until now we have only been viewing half of the Motion tab, which is the controls section, it is now time to explore the other half of the facility which is where individual keyframes are plotted on horizontal lines. The plotted points – keyframes – represent moves which are animated over time.

1   Set up the interface as illustrated.

2   Make sure you have two layers of video in the Timeline – one shot on top of another.

3   Position the Scrubber Bar on the first frame of the Sequence and turn your attention to the Canvas. The video of layer 2 will be all you see for

the moment. Using the pointer double click the second video track in the Timeline to make it active in the Viewer.

4   Click on the Motion tab in the Viewer.

▼ Basic Motion	
Scale	◄ ⁴¹🏠┈┈┈┈┈┈┈┈► 45

5   Use the Scale control to reduce the image in size.

6   Select Image 1 Wireframe mode from the pull-down menu in the Canvas. Click in the center of the image and drag the image to the left where you want the effect to begin.

Image

✓ Image+Wireframe

Wireframe

Resize and Reposition the Image

7   Click with the yellow Scrubber Bar in the Timeline/Canvas and position it where you want the effect to begin.

Video	Mono (a1)	Mono (a2)	Filters	Motion
Name		Parameters		Nav
▼ Basic Motion				⊗ ☑▾
Scale		◄ ⁴¹🏠┈┈┈┈┈┈► 50		◁◈▷

Insert/Delete Keyframe

8   Press the Insert/Delete Keyframe button in the Motion Control tab of the Viewer next to the word Scale. This will set the first keyframe.

9   Use the controls in the Motion tab to rotate the image counterclockwise. You can type in a numeric value if you prefer.

10 Press the Insert/Delete Keyframe button again – to the right of the word Rotate. This will add a rotation value to the effect.

11 Press the Insert/Delete Keyframe button once more – this time next to Center. This is a positioning or location reference point.

Video	Mono (a1)	Mono (a2)	Filters	Motion		
Name		Parameters			Nav	00;00
▼ Basic Motion		Master Reset Button			⊗ ☑ ▾	◀▶
Scale		◀ ┌─☖─┼─┼─┼─┼─┼─┐ ▶		50	◀ ◈ ▶	◆
Rotation		┌─⊘─┐		-10	◀ ◈ ▶	482 ◆ -432
Center		⊕	-238.58 ,	-91.07	◀ ◈ ▶	◆

All these points add up to one keyframe – a combination of size, rotation and positioning. The first keyframe is now marked.

12 Reposition the yellow Scrubber Bar where you want the next keyframe point to be marked. You will notice that the yellow Scrubber Bar moves in three places at once – in the Timeline, Canvas and Motion tab window.

13 Click in the center of the image and drag it to the right. A line indicating the path the image will follow will be displayed.

14 Resize the image by using the Scale controls in the Motion Control tab. The second keyframe points are automatically added as Scale, Rotation and the Center are adjusted. This is represented visually in the Motionwindow by the line which gradually rises to indicate the move which has been plotted.

Resize, Rotate and Reposition the Image

Name	Parameters	Nav	00:00
▼ Basic Motion		⊗ ☑▾	◆——————⊣
Scale	◄ ▫▫▫⌐▫▫▫▫▫▫ ► [70]	◄ ◈ ▷	◇————————◇
Rotation	– ⌀ – [-12]	◄ ◈ ▷	432 / ◇ / -432
Center	⊕ [70.3 , [-130.2]	◄ ◈ ▷	◆————◆

Use These Arrows to Jump between Keyframes

15 Rotate the image using the Rotation control in the Motion tab window. The second keyframe is added automatically for rotation.

You now have two keyframes plotted and this is represented visually by the dots marked on the right side of the Motion Control window. You can jump back and forth between the two keyframes by using the forward and backward arrows next to the Insert/Delete Keyframe buttons in the Motion Control window.

Playback the effect, providing the RT Extreme settings allow. Otherwise you will need to render to see the result.

			Viewer: Balloon Lands from Sequence 16
Video / Mono (a1) / Mono (a2) / Filters / **Motion**			
Name	Parameters	Nav	00:00 01:00:00
▼ Basic Motion		⊗ ☑▾	◆————————◆————⊣
Scale	◄ ▫▫▫⌐▫▫▫▫▫ ► [110]	◄ ◈ ▷	◇————◇————◇
Rotation	– ⌀ – [0]	◄ ◈ ▷	432 / ◇————◇ / -432
Center	⊕ [315.27 , [-107.44]	◄ ◈ ▷	◆————◆————◆

16 We are just about there. Move the Scrubber Bar forward to the final keyframe point. Adjust the Scale, Rotation and Center controls. Keyframe points for each of these will be added automatically with each adjustment.

It should be clear that a distinct set of processes is being followed each time a keyframe is added. The image needs to be sized using the controls in the Motion tab; rotated and positioned. The first keyframe must be added manually, by pressing the Insert/Delete Keyframe button, while each keyframe thereafter is added automatically each time an adjustment is made to any of the parameters.

The duration of the effect is determined by the distance or separation between the first and last keyframe. The process is logical and straightforward. It is crucial not to miss out any of the steps as this will interrupt the effect you are trying to create.

By dragging the Scrubber Bar through the effect in either the Canvas or the Timeline you can see the path the effect will follow. Playback the result through RT Extreme or render the effect, if need be. Check to see if you are happy with it. If not, repeat the process and try again.

Keyframe points can be smoothed by Control clicking on the keyframe point itself.

Note: Keyframes can easily be reset by clicking the Reset button at the top of the Motion Control tab. Keyframes can be deleted by pressing the Insert/Delete Keyframe button. If a keyframe already exists it will be deleted. If there is no keyframe present one will be added. Another way to delete keyframes is to select the Pen tool from the Toolbar, position it over a keyframe point and hold down the Alt/Option key (which gives you a minus symbol). By clicking on any of the keyframe points they will be deleted.

Keyframes can also be repositioned by dragging. Simply position your cursor over a keyframe point and your cursor will turn into a small cross. Drag the keyframe to a new position and release it.

You may notice that when you drag the yellow Scrubber Bar, it moves in the Timeline, the Canvas and the Motion Control area all at the same time. Each of these areas is linked, thus adjustments to one area affect the other areas.

Should you wish for the box to start outside of frame you need to reduce the size of the Canvas using the drop down % menu at the top of the Canvas.

This will resize the overall size of the frame inside the Canvas giving you the flexibility of adding keyframes outside of the television viewing area.

By reducing the overall display to either 12% or 25% it is possible to have animated objects fly in and out of frame from the top, bottom or either side of frame. By working with several layers of video one can animate several boxes at a time. The same can be achieved with text or imported Photoshop files.

When you really know what you are doing you can make the illusion complete.

Multi-Layered Dissolves

Cuts and dissolves are the bread and butter of filmmaking. Effects have always been a luxury, however, with the availability of effects which don't cost money there has been a huge increase in what clients and producers demand. It seems as if everyone wants to add extra shine to what might otherwise be a mediocre film. While overuse of effects will fail to make a bad production good – tasteful use of effects can be pleasing to the eye and if nothing else provides visual interest. The term 'eye candy' has been used to describe many of the effects offered in desktop editing systems.

A dissolve is nothing more than one shot fading into another. By placing a third layer over a dissolve it is possible to create what is known as the three-way dissolve. In the world of film production one had to plan dissolves, send the negative to the lab and hope the result was something close to what was envisaged. When using Final Cut Pro you can experiment to your heart's content. You can even create four, five and six layer dissolves and beyond. The result can end up being a mash of unwatchable imagery – so be careful.

To create a three-way dissolve is not difficult:

1   Make sure you have three empty video tracks in the Timeline.

2   Layer two clips on top of each other – the third layer will be added later.

3   Make sure Clip Overlays is switched on.

4   Adjust the opacity of the video clips on V1 and V2 to achieve the result you are after. This is achieved by moving the black line inside the clip in the Timeline up and down. Providing the yellow Scrubber Bar is positioned within the bounds of the two clips the result will be displayed in the Canvas.

5   Once you are happy with the result add the third layer of video to V3.

6   Adjust the opacity, using Clip Overlays, until you can see all three images bleeding through. You may need to make further adjustments to 'get it right'.

7   If necessary, render to check you are happy with the result.

8   Select the Pen tool from the very bottom of the Toolbar.

9   Point your cursor at the black line of the base video clip. Your cursor will turn into a pen.

10 Click on the black line and a point will be added. This will be your first keyframe.

11 Add another keyframe to the left. By allowing your cursor to hover over either keyframes you will see it turns into a cross.

12 Drag the keyframe on the left to the base of the clip.

13 Perform the same function to the other clips, dragging keyframes to the base of the clip. What you are doing is plotting points so that the images will fade in and out at your discretion.

14 Once you feel you have the points correctly plotted, render, if you need to, and then play back the result. You may need to make further adjustments if the result is not as you wish it to be.

If you follow points 1–7 you will achieve the result of a three-way superimposition. This may be fine for your purposes. If, however, you want the images to fade in and out at predefined points you need to use the Pen tool to plot keyframes. It is possible to have a single image play, have another image dissolve over it to be followed by a third image. I'm a big fan of three-way dissolves. They can look great and produce subtle or high impact results depending on how they are treated. The interface within Final Cut Pro is particularly suited to this type of work. The hassles required in a tape suite to achieve these effects were enough to persuade many editors never to try. As for the film world – now that would have been really difficult.

Keyframing Filters

Just as Motion can be keyframed, Filters can also be keyframed. By definition keyframing means to change over time. Therefore Filters can be animated over time in a similar way to keyframing Motion Effects.

1   Add a Filter to a clip by dragging it from the Effects tab onto a clip in the Timeline. I suggest using a Gaussian Blur for the purpose of this exercise. Make sure the clip you are working with is no shorter than 10 seconds in duration.

2   Make sure the Pointer tool is selected. Double click the clip in the Timeline to which the Filter has been added. This will make the clip active in the Viewer.

3   Position the yellow Scrubber Bar on the beginning of the clip in the Timeline.

			Viewer: Sun Over Highway 2 from Sequence
Video	Mono (a1)	Mono (a2)	Filters	Motion
Name	Parameters		Nav	01:00:45:00
▼ Video Filters				
▼ ✔ Gaussian...			⊗ ☑ ▾	
Channel	Alpha+RGB			
Radius	◁———————▸	0	◁ ◉ ▷	
▼ Mono 1 Filters				

4   Select the Filters tab in the Viewer. This will reveal the controls for changing the settings of the Filter you are working with.

5   Make sure the setting for the filter effect is at 0. This will mean the Filter will have no effect on the clip at this stage.

6   Mark a keyframe by pressing the Insert/Delete Keyframe button.

7   Move the Scrubber Bar several seconds into the clip (by holding down the Shift key + the

Ins/Del Keyframe

horizontal forward arrow you can skip forward one second at a time). Do not adjust the Filter settings yet.

8   Mark another keyframe. You will now have two keyframes marked.

9   Move the Scrubber Bar forward several more seconds.

10   Adjust the Filter settings to bring the clip completely out of focus.

What you have effectively done is place a filter on a clip in the Timeline and mark three keyframes to it. The first and second keyframes are marked with the filter set to zero, thus it has no effect on the clip – this ensures when the clip plays, initially there is no visual change to its appearance. The third keyframe is added where the filter settings are adjusted to bring the clip out of focus. Thus when the clip plays, initially it is in focus until the third keyframe where it moves out of focus. This is a simple and easy way to simulate a pull focus.

By using the above method you can keyframe many of the filters found under the Effects tab. For example, you could keyframe a clip so that the appearance changes from full color to black and white – or vice versa. You could keyframe a clip using the Fisheye filter so that it appears normal and over time changes as if it is being distorted by an extreme wide angle lens. The possibilities are endless. Through keyframing one has access to powerful tools to change the look, shape and feel of clips.

Time Remapping

Time Remapping is an easy and effective technique for performing what is called 'ramping' of speed. You can 'ramp' from slow to fast, fast to slow, slow to fast to slow, and into reverse or forwards motion at will.

In essence to work with the Time Remap feature is not difficult. It involves setting keyframes and moving these keyframes to create a shift in time, within the confines of the overall length of the clip. It is important to understand when using this function that the overall duration of a clip remains exactly the same. When slowing down or speeding up clips using the conventional speed modifier, found under the Modify menu, the duration of a clip is made longer for slow motion or shorter for fast motion. When using Time Remap the clip stays the same in length, it is the motion within the start and end points of the clip that are affected.

Before beginning work I suggested you set up your Viewer and Browser for compositing mode – that is spread out the Viewer so that you have access to the second half where keyframes can be plotted.

1 Double click the clip in the Timeline you wish to work with. This will open the shot into the Viewer.

2 Click the Motion tab in the Viewer.

3 Click the arrow next to Time Remap and scroll down to reveal the graph on the right-hand side.

163

4   Click the Toggle Keyframes button at the bottom
left of the Timeline. This will alter the visual
appearance of the Timeline vertically. You will see
increment steps below each of the clips in the Timeline.

The Time
Remap Tool

5   Choose the Time Remap tool from the
Toolbar.

6   Click with the Time Remap tool at two
points within the clip you wish to alter.
This will plot two keyframes in the line
below the clip. There will now be a total
of four keyframes marked – one at the
beginning, two in the middle and one at
the end of the clip.

Notice that the line in the graph moves from bottom to top in a continuous angle. Look to the Timeline, below the clips, and you will see that there are equally spaced increments. Both the continuous angle and the equally spaced increments indicate that the speed within the clip is constant.

Let me repeat this. If the increments are evenly spaced then speed is constant. Now for the other part of the equation – if the increments are spread out then time will be in slow motion and if the increments are close together the result is fast motion.

Slow Motion **Fast Motion**

1   Select the Time Remap tool and allow it to hover within the clip, above one of the keyframe points in the center of the Timeline. The tool will turn into a + symbol.

2   Click on the keyframe and move it to either side. Watch what happens to the marked increments beneath the clip (it may be advisable to increase the spread within the Timeline to get a better look at the result). You will notice the increments contract and expand as you

move the points. Thus, you can create an effect where a clip will begin in slow motion, speed up

and then slow down again at the end of the clip. The plotting of keyframes is reflected in the graph in the Motion tab.

You can also move the keyframe points within the Motion window. Make sure you have selected the Time Remap tool and simply grab hold of the keyframes and move them. Keep an eye on the increments in the Timeline beneath the clip and observe whether they contract or expand. Remember, spread apart will create slow motion, whereas increments close together will create fast motion.

If you want a clip to play forward then into reverse you need to plot the keyframes so that the angle within the graphical display in the Motion tab is straight up and down.

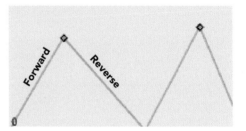

A line climbing at an angle vertically indicates forwards motion, while a line heading downhill is for reverse. You can therefore set a clip to move forwards, backwards and forwards with each move effectively ramping time into slow or fast motion.

One final tip: if you control click on any of the keyframes in the Motion tab you will get an option to clear a keyframe or make it smooth. Select the smooth option and play back the result. You can perform Time Remapping functions at keyframe points which are smooth and fluid. This is a great way to make variations in motion flow in a subtle way.

Experiment with Time Remapping by using two, three, four and more keyframes. What I have described is a basic way to get this function to work. Now it is up to you to build on this.

Copy and Pasting Attributes

When you work hard at building a set of effects it can be a great timesaver to be able to copy the settings from one clip to another. For example, you may wish to run a series of clips in slow motion at 35%. Rather than setting the speed for each clip individually, it can be quicker to set this up for a single clip and to then copy the slow motion setting from one clip to all the others you wish to slow down. Details can be copied and pasted for many settings including: opacity, cropping, motion, drop shadows, filters and motion blur.

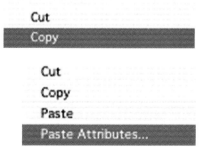

1   Control click in the Timeline on a clip from which you wish to copy the attributes. This will open a menu with many options. Select Copy.

2   Move your cursor to the clip you wish to paste the attributes to. Control click on this clip and select Paste Attributes from the menu.

3   Another menu will now open. Choose the options you wish to apply to the clip. Do this by checking the boxes with a tick. Obviously, the only attributes which you can apply are those which were already applied to the clip from which the attributes were copied.

Titling

As an all round editing package Final Cut Pro covers virtually every area a filmmaker will ever need to explore. No film would be complete without Titles. If nothing else a simple opening caption to identify a production is required. Final Cut Pro does much more than this including Moving Titles, Transparent Shadows and Animated Text.

Some of these operations can be quite complex, however, the basics are not difficult to master.

To access Titling in Final Cut Pro go to the Effects tab and locate Video Generators.

1   Click the triangle to the left of Video Generators to reveal a list of options.

2   Click the triangle next to Text – this will reveal a list of possible options to choose from.

Note: for really fancy titles look towards Livetype which is separate application bundled with Final Cut Studio. Livetype is specifically designed for complex text creation and is fully capable of making titles comparable to those seen on network television.

For the moment choose the fifth option – Text.

3   Click on the Text Generator and drag it onto the V2 track in the Timeline where you want the Text to be positioned. Make sure you release it with a vertical arrow pointing downwards, thus performing an Overwrite Edit.

4   Double click the Text Generator on the second video track – this will load the Text into the Viewer. If your computer is capable of RT Extreme a green line will sit above the line of text in the Timeline indicating the result will play in real time. Otherwise, you will see a red line indicating that rendering is required.

5 In the Viewer click once on the second tab at the top – Controls.

6 Make sure the Scrubber Bar in the Timeline is positioned on the shot which has the Text Generator positioned above it. This ensures the result will be displayed in the Canvas as you work.

7 You should now see the words 'Sample Text' in the Canvas.

8 Return to the Viewer – make sure you have clicked the Controls tab – click in the box to highlight the words 'Sample Text'. Overtype 'Sample Text' with whatever text you wish to enter.

9 Click in the Timeline again and nudge the Scrubber Bar a few frames along using the arrow keys – the text will appear in the Canvas, over the shot where the Scrubber Bar is positioned.

Font	Futura
Size	
Style	Plain
Alignment	Center
Font Color	
Origin	0 ,
Tracking	
Leading	
Aspect	
Auto Kerning	☑
Use Subpixel	☑

10 You can modify the characteristics of the text by adjusting the details in the Controls area. You can change the font, the size, the color and tracking by altering each of the parameters.

11 To reposition the text click on the '1' symbol in the Controls area labelled Origin. Click once on the '1' symbol and a small '+' will appear in the Canvas.

12 Clicking in the Canvas window sets the '+' wherever you click with the mouse button. Release your mouse button at the location where you want the text to be repositioned. Alternatively, you can enter X and Y co-ordinates in the Origin area in the Controls window.

Another way to move the text around is to switch on Image + Wireframe. Click with your mouse in the center of the active text window and you can then freely position the text with the mouse.

There are other Text Generators available. These include Outline Text, Crawl, Typewriter and Scrolling Text. All of these are variations on the basic Text Generator we have been working with. Experiment with these to see what they do and how they work. It is also possible to layer text, as with video tracks, so that several different layers of text can be built in different styles.

The easiest way to add a drop shadow is to go into the Motion window and switch Drop Shadow on. You need to make sure that the text generator is loaded into and active in the Viewer for this to work. You can then alter the direction, color, opacity and size of the drop shadow.

The quickest way to alter the overall opacity of the text is the same as with other clips in the Timeline. Simply switch on Clip Overlays and drop the black line inside of the text generator in the Timeline to adjust the overall opacity.

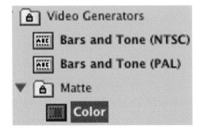

To position text over a colored background select Matte from within Generators (found under the Effects tab in the Browser). You then need to overlay the Matte Color on top of the video track and then position the Text Generator of your choice over this.

The Matte Generator can be cropped in the Motion window and the transparency adjusted through either the opacity setting in the Motion window or by using Clip Overlays. Professional looking titles can then be achieved.

Switch on the Safe Title display to show what is termed 'cutoff'. This is found under the same menu as Image + Wireframe.

Master Templates

One can tap directly into the power of Motion from within Final Cut Pro 6 through the Master Templates. This is advantageous as the editor can access these effects without having to step outside of the Final Cut Pro environment – thus there is no need to learn another application. These templates work in a very similar way to the other effects in Final Cut Pro.

There are four ways to access the Master Templates:

1 through the Effects tab in the Browser of Final Cut Pro

2 through the drop-down area in the Viewer where one accesses the Generators

3 through the drop-down in the Viewer where one accesses the Generators

4 One can also choose the Sequence Menu and scroll to the Add Master Template command for a full visual view of available templates (see end of this chapter).

Note that the Master Templates are format specific and it is therefore important that you choose the template which corresponds to the format you are working with. Templates are available for HD, NTSC or PAL. You will need the Motion content files installed to make use of these templates.

1 Choose a Template by either double-clicking in the Effects tab of the Browser or by scrolling and releasing your mouse button in the Effects menu or the area at the bottom of the Viewer. Wait a moment and the Master Template will then open in the Viewer.

2 Press the Space Bar to preview the effect. You may wish to run through several effects until you find what you are looking for. You can then edit this effect into the Timeline using Insert or Overwrite – or continue working inside the Viewer and then edit the effect into the Timeline later.

3 Go to the Controls tab in the Viewer – it is here that you can modify the text and place video into the various Drop Zones or Wells which are provided.

4 Drag video from the Browser into the Drop Zones of the Template you are working with. Not all the Templates provide Drop Zones – some are designed as lower text captions and will only provide parameters to change text.

5 Overtype the text and adjust the size using the sliders provided. If you have edited the Template into the Timeline, which I would recommend, you will then see the result in the Canvas, provided that the yellow scrubber bar is positioned on the effect.

6   Render the effect or play back through Dynamic RT if your computer is up to it.

Note: when working with 'lower third' templates these provide what is known as a key signal. This means one can see through to the video on a layer below that to which the effect has been placed.

The Master Templates provide a quick and easy way to create great looking graphics without having to spend hours learning another application or fine tuning the result.

One can alter the size and tracking of text and also keyframe text attributes though the movement of text and video is restricted to the preset moves. While you are locked into the programmed movies do not dismiss these effects as gimmicks. Using the Master Templates enables one to produce visual animations which compare to network television graphics, and provide a means for anyone to access the power of Motion without having to learn the application.

If you want to take these effects further then step into Motion where full customization is possible.

Sequence Effects Tools

Render Selection
Render All
Render Only

Settings...

Lift
Ripple Delete
Close Gap
Solo Selected Item(s)
Nest Item(s)...

Add Edit
Extend Edit
Add Video Transition
Add Audio Transition
Transition Alignment
Trim Edit

Add Master Template...

Insert Tracks...
Delete Tracks...

All Master Templates

If one chooses the Sequence menu and scrolls down to the Add Master Template command, you will then be offered a visual view of the Master Templates which are categorised according to themes. One can easily get an overview of HD templates, widescreen, standard, PAL, NTSC, bumpers, lower thirds, transitions and openers. It is like having a one box solution to make up graphics for many different uses.

Click the folder All Master Templates and you can see as visual icons all the Master Templates which can be used.

Double-click the template of choice and you can then integrate the moving graphics into your production.

AUDIO

The application grows as you grow.
ABBA SHAPIRO
WASHINGTON DC FINAL CUT PRO USER GROUP

It's been said before that audiences will more readily accept bad images when watching a film than they will accept bad audio. Out of focus, jerky, misframed shots, in limited doses, will not cause a viewer to switch off. Bad sound, on the other hand, will turn the film experience into a torturous ordeal. If the audience can't hear what is going on, or if the content simply hurts their ears, then it is very difficult to maintain their attention.

The only way to get good sound is to record it properly in the first place. Basic rules to achieve this include: using good microphones; getting the microphone as close to the subject's mouth as possible; listening to the sound through headphones as it is recorded and setting the audio levels correctly. The likelihood is, if it sounds good at the time of recording then it will sound good in the edit suite.

Setting Correct Audio Levels

Audio levels are crucial to get right. If you set the level too high you will blow it, literally. When digital audio peaks too loud the sound will distort, break up and be unlistenable. Often called 'pumping' this will sound far worse in a digital environment than it would have in the analog world.

The basic rule with recording sound is don't let the audio meters push into the red. This applies for recording audio on location and working with sound in the edit suite. Many experts advise that DV audio should peak no louder than −12 dB. I tend to allow my audio to peak between −12 dB and −6 dB and don't experience any problems.

Working with audio in the digital domain is different to working analog. When it was all phono jacks and speaker wire one would push the audio so that it peaked high (obviously not to the point of distortion). With digital it is recommended to keep audio levels lower rather than higher. When digital distorts you really know about it. It doesn't just break up; it completely breaks up. By keeping the levels lower, rather than louder in a digital environment, you are less likely to experience problems.

Getting the Most Out of your Audio

Once your audio is recorded you are more or less stuck with it. While it is possible to improve the quality through use of filters and other means, in general the quality is determined by what is recorded on tape in the first place. However, within Final Cut Pro there are several features which enable you to put together a good sound mix. The sound mix refers to the way all of the elements blend together to create the overall soundtrack.

To produce an integrated soundtrack which is both seamless and effective one needs to be able to adjust audio levels and to program smooth fades and mix several tracks of audio together. Final Cut Pro allows the editor to adjust and mix audio levels in real time and it does a very good job of this.

To mix audio effectively I strongly suggest that you work with what is known as Stereo Pairs. Once captured, clips can be converted into Stereo Pairs.

Converting Clips into Stereo Pairs

Each clip that you capture is made up of two tracks – a left track and a right track. When mixing these tracks, unless you are working on a complex sound mix with defined stereo separation, it is useful to marry these audio tracks together so that any adjustments to audio levels will apply to both tracks. Otherwise, when you adjust the audio levels you will need to make sure that each track is adjusted by exactly the same amount – a difficult and time-consuming process.

You can tell if your clips are Stereo Pairs by looking at the audio tracks in the Timeline. A Stereo Pair is defined by two sets of triangles facing each other. If these triangles are present then you are working with Stereo Pairs – if there 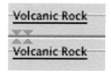 are no triangles present you need to convert your tracks into Stereo Pairs.

1 Select the horizontal Arrow tool in the Toolbar and highlight the entire contents of the Timeline.

2 Choose the pull down menu at the top of the screen titled Modify. Scroll to Stereo Pair and release your mouse button. This toggles to Stereo Pair. A tick means Stereo Pair is selected. By selecting Stereo Pair you are instructing Final Cut Pro to convert whichever clips you have highlighted.

3 All your clips should now be converted to Stereo Pairs. You can confirm this by checking that two sets of triangles facing each other are present in each of the audio tracks. Providing these triangles are present then your audio has been converted into Stereo Pairs.

Note: the shortcut to convert clips into Stereo Pairs is **Alt/Option + L**. This can be done for a single or multiple highlighted clips.

It is important to listen to the sound of the clips once they are converted. Then compare the sound to the clips before they were converted to Stereo Pairs. I have experienced, on some occasions, times when clips sound better as non-stereo pairs. To compare simply convert a clip to a Stereo Pair, and listen to it.

Press **Apple Z** to undo the conversion.

Press **Apple Shift Z** to redo the command.

Adjusting Audio Levels

1   Click on the Clip Overlays symbol at the bottom left of the
Timeline.

2   A pink line appears in each of the audio tracks and a black line in the
video track. You will be familiar with Clip Overlays from the effects
section.

3   Point your cursor at the pink lines. When you get
close to these lines your cursor turns into two short
horizontal lines with vertical arrows on either side.

4   Click your mouse button and you can now move the pink lines up or
down. If you move the lines up the volume for the clip will increase, if
you move the lines down the volume will decrease. Providing you
converted the clips into stereo pairs the lines will move together as you
make adjustments. Using this method it is possible to balance any
differences in audio levels between clips to achieve a smooth and
natural sound mix.

As you make adjustments, keep an eye on the audio levels on the meters
within Final Cut Pro or, if you are working with a deck or a camera, on the
meters on the external device.

Boosting Audio Levels with the Audio Gain Filter

If you find you cannot get enough level by pushing the pink line to the top
of the clip then drop the Gain filter onto the clip you are working with.
Simply access this from the Effects area in the folder titled Audio Filters – Final

Cut Pro. The maximum increase in volume when using the pink lines is 12 dB while when using the Gain filter, introduced with Final Cut Pro 6, one can increase the volume by close to 100 dB.

1   Click the Effects Tab in the Browser and scroll to Audio Filters.

2   Click the arrow next to Final Cut Pro and click to select the Gain filter.

3   Drag the Gain filter to the audio tracks you wish to adjust.

4   Double click the clip to make it active in the Viewer and click the Filters tab to view the controls – if it is a stereo pair you are working with, the Gain filter will affect both tracks and you will have a single slider to work with; if your clip has two audio tracks which are not stereo pairs then two independent sliders will provide separate control for each audio track.

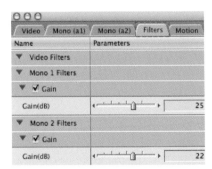

Stereo Pairs   **Non-Stereo Pairs**

5 Use the slider to increase the volume and move the slider, while playing back the audio live, to hear the increase in level, keeping your eyes on the audio meters while you work. If you adjust the level while playing the clip the increase or decrease will be plotted as keyframes.

If you wish to increase the level by the same amount for several clips in the Timeline first add the Gain filter to a single clip, increase the level to the desired amount, then control-click the clip and

select Copy. Highlight the other clips you wish to affect – control-click these and choose Paste Attributes. Check Filters in Audio Attributes and click OK to apply. The parameters you set in the first clip will then be applied to those clips you have highlighted.

While it is most useful to be able to adjust audio levels using the methods described the requirements of most productions go far beyond being able to increase and decrease the sound levels. One needs to be able to include smooth fades and

185

cross fades to build an audio mix where each of the elements blends together in a perfect mix of sound effects, narration and music.

Adding Sound Fades

There are two ways to add audio fades to the tracks in the Timeline. You can manually plot keyframes, using the technique known as Rubberbanding. Alternatively, the audio mixer can be used to alter the levels. Shifts in levels, using the audio mixer, can be recorded as keyframes which can then be manipulated in the Timeline.

To keyframe fades directly into the Timeline requires a similar process as adding keyframes to effects in the Motion Control window.

1   Make sure Clip Overlays is switched on and make sure all the clips in the Timeline have been converted to Stereo Pairs.

2   Select the Pen tool at the very bottom of the Toolbar.

3   Point your cursor at the pink lines and the cursor will turn into the Pen tool. Choose a point on the pink lines where you wish for the sound fade to begin and click with your mouse. A pink dot will be marked. This mark is a keyframe and represents the beginning of the fade (the keyframe will apply to both audio tracks in the Stereo Pair).

4   If you want to reposition the keyframe, point the cursor at the keyframe mark and the cursor now becomes a small cross. Click once, with the small cross on the keyframe. You can now move the keyframe by dragging.

If you wish to delete the keyframe hold down the Alt key and the Pen tool will now have a minus symbol next to it. If you click on the keyframe with the minus symbol the keyframe will be deleted. The Pen tool with a minus symbol can also be selected from the Tool Palette by extending the Pen tools and choosing the second option.

5   Add a second keyframe further along in the clip. You should now have two keyframes marked. To create an audio fade at least two keyframes are required.

6   Hold the Pen tool over the first keyframe so that the tool becomes a small cross. Use the little cross to drag the first keyframe down to the base of the clip. You should now have a curved line which starts at the bottom of the clip and rises in a curve to the top of the second keyframe. Play back the clip and your sound will rise from silence at the first mark to a defined volume at the second mark.

For fine adjustments hold down the Shift key while dragging the keyframes up or down.

It is useful when working with audio to increase the size of the Timeline vertically, thus giving a better view of any adjustments you make. This is achieved by clicking on the small boxes located on the bottom left-hand side of the Timeline. Choose whichever size you feel most comfortable with.

It can also be useful to increase the overall horizontal size of the Timeline. Use the Magnifier tool to achieve this or pull on the ribbed ends of the slider bar at the base of the Timeline. This allows for fine adjustments to be made to the audio over time.

Increase the Spread of the Timeline for Fine Control

The Audio Mixer

Built into Final Cut Pro is the facility known as the Audio Mixer. This can be easily accessed from the Tools menu; alternatively select the Easy Setup titled Audio Mixing. This will set up the Final Cut Pro interface with the Audio Mixer conveniently positioned above the Timeline and to the right of the Viewer and Canvas.

The Audio Mixer allows you to visually mix your tracks, enabling you to smooth out differences in levels and to program smooth fades and shifts in volume. In essence, it performs similar functions to the Rubberbanding technique, but in

a more intuitive and user friendly way. I work between Rubberbanding and the Audio Mixer in creating my mixes.

The Audio Mixer has been designed to resemble a true hardware mixer. The major difference is that it is only possible to mix a single track at a time, or two tracks if they have been converted into Stereo Pairs. With a true hardware mixer it is possible to mix several tracks, due to the fact that as humans we have ten fingers to work with and can, thus, mix several faders at a time.

This, however, is not a huge disadvantage, because it is possible to record audio keyframes, thus tracks can be mixed individually, the results recorded, and then played back while further mixing takes place.

The audio mixer is made up of several virtual faders, stacked from left to right to represent each of the tracks in the Timeline. If you have four tracks in the Timeline the audio mixer will have four faders; if you have ten audio tracks there will be ten faders for you to access in the mixer. Above each fader is a pan control, allowing you to shift the playback of audio from left to right. Tracks can be easily muted or soloed using the speaker or headphone icons. A master stereo fader is positioned to the right of the faders which controls the overall output level. A master mute button is positioned above the master fader.

A set of Audio Meters is positioned next to the Master Fader. This serves the same purpose as the Audio Meters which sit to the right of the Timeline.

To the extreme left of the Audio Mixer are radio buttons which can be used to selectively hide tracks from view. This can be useful if you are working with many tracks at a time. You may wish to hide tracks to concentrate on those you are focusing on at any given time.

The killer feature of this mixer is the Record Audio Keyframes button, located at the top right of the mixer above the Master Mute button. The Record Audio Keyframes button is used to plot points in the Timeline, in a similar way to Rubberbanding, however, the difference is the points are plotted in real time as the sound is mixed. Once these points have been plotted you can then get inside the mix, providing Keyframe Overlays is switched on, and make manual adjustments as necessary.

Final Cut Pro File
About Final Cut Pro

User Preferences...

The amount of keyframes plotted by the Record Audio Keyframes button is adjustable. Click the Final Cut Pro menu, scroll to User Preferences and choose the Editing Tab.

To the right is the Record Audio Keyframes command.

Record Audio Keyframes:
All
Reduced
Peaks Only

From the drop-down menu are three choices: All, Reduced or Peaks Only.

All Audio Keyframes   Reduced Audio Keyframes

Adjusting and Recording Audio Keyframes

1 Position the yellow Scrubber Bar at the beginning of the section of audio you wish to mix.

2 Click the Record Audio Keyframes button at the top of the mixer. The button will change from gray to green indicating that it is now active.

3 Play the Sequence and adjust the fader, or set of two faders which are linked as Stereo Pairs, and mix the sound in real time.

4 When you have finished your mix press the Space Bar to stop. Press the Record Audio Keyframes button to switch it off. This is important, as it is possible to inadvertently record over your mix.

If you are happy with the result carry on working, otherwise you can choose to make slight adjustments inside the Timeline using the Rubberbanding technique, or remix if necessary.

I find it useful to mix a single track at a time, or a set of Stereo Pairs, and then to repeat the procedure on another set of Stereo Pairs, or individual tracks, if necessary.

The audio level of each of the individual tracks can be raised or lowered with the Record Audio Keyframes facility switched off. Simply move the faders up or down for any adjustments. This is a quick way to bump up the level or to drop the level and provides a convenient alternative to using Clip Overlays to achieve the same result.

Adding Audio Cross Fades

Audio Cross Fades are used for creating seamless blends between Audio Transitions. All sorts or unwanted sounds can be easily eliminated.

1 Select the Effects tab located top right of the Browser.

2 Scroll down to Audio Transitions – click on the triangle to the left to reveal the contents.

3 Click on Cross Fade (0dB) and drag this to the cut point between the two audio tracks where you want the Cross Fade to occur.

4 Playback the section with the Cross Fade and decide whether you are happy with the result. If you wish to change the duration double click on the Cross Fade which is positioned at the cut point between the two clips. This will open a dialog box, which will allow you to enter a new duration. Enter the duration and click OK.

The result should be a nice smooth Cross Fade where one section of audio blends into another.

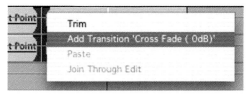

Audio Cross Fades can also be added by positioning the yellow Scrubber Bar at an edit point and choosing the Effects menu at the top of the screen. Choose one of the Audio Transitions.

A third way to add Audio Cross Fades is to Control click at an edit point between two clips. The option will be given to add a cross dissolve if you click in the video track or to add a cross fade if you click in either one of the audio tracks.

Adding Audio Tracks

Audio tracks can be added or deleted in the same way as video tracks. Simply hold down the Control key and click in the gray area of the Timeline next to the audio symbols. A menu will open giving you the option to add or delete a track.

Remember to add two tracks for each section of stereo audio required.

Just as video tracks can be dragged directly into the Timeline the same applies to audio tracks. If you wish to add a CD track, for example, which you have already imported into the Browser, then drag the track directly from the Browser into the Timeline. If the item is dragged to an already existing audio

track you will get the result of an Insert Edit if your cursor points to the top third of the track. An Overwrite Edit will occur if your cursor points to the bottom half.

Insert Edit   **Overwrite Edit**

Audio tracks can be added to the Timeline by dragging a CD track directly from the Browser to the gray area in the Timeline below the last existing audio track.

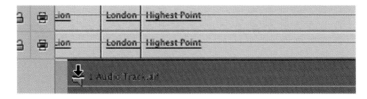

The CD track will then be added and two new tracks created to accommodate it.

This is the quickest way to create new tracks and at the same time get a new piece of audio into the Timeline. If you wish you can then delete the audio and these tracks will remain free to be used however you wish.

Mixdown Audio

If you work with more audio tracks than your computer can comfortably play then you may choose to invoke the Mixdown Audio command.

1   Select the Sequence menu and scroll to Render Only.

2   Move right and down until you get to Mixdown.

The Mixdown command can also be accessed by pressing Apple + Alt/Option + R.

This will mix all your audio tracks into a single file. Everything will appear exactly the same in the Timeline, however, Final Cut Pro will reference to a single file. This is useful if you are working with a complex audio mix which involves more tracks than your computer can mix in real time.

The downside to using the Mixdown Audio command is that each time you change the edits in the Timeline you will need to do another mixdown. Unless you are working with many tracks of audio, or use a lot of audio filters, keyframes or effects, you may never need to use this function.

I can't tell you how amazed I was when I did my first output from Final
Cut Pro in the living room of my apartment. And I was dancing all
around the room just as happy as can be.
KEVIN MONAHAN
SF CUTTERS

Once your production is complete it is time to output your movie.

The simplest form of output is to roll record on your camera or deck and then play the movie direct from the Timeline and straight to tape. This is something you should do regularly throughout the editing process to ensure you have a backup of your film should a technical catastrophe or any other sort of problem render your project useless.

When working with DV I always back up my material to digital tape in the form of several different versions: with and without graphics and effects and with separate audio tracks, both mixed and unmixed. One pass may include voiceover, another music, and another sound effects. By doing backups in this way all of the raw elements of the film are preserved so that in the event of a corrupt file, human error, or power failure, you will be able to rebuild your film from the elements recorded to tape. It takes discipline to back up your work regularly, however, unless you have tremendous amounts of hard drive space, so that you can afford a true backup of all of the project files in the form of data, then backing up to digital tape is the best option.

Print to Video

Print to Video is a function Apple built into Final Cut Pro to give a professional look to a finished film. Here the project can be named, color bars can be inserted at the head and black can be added at the end of the production. It is also possible to loop the film so that several copies can be recorded onto a single digital tape, or one can choose to record sections of the movie by defining 'in' and 'out' points and only printing these sections to tape.

Print to Video also serves another purpose. If any material is unrendered then the computer will render this material prior to invoking the Print to Video command and if your audio mix is complex then a mixdown will take place. This ensures all the components of your production should play without problem. Sometimes dropped frames may be encountered during normal playback and the problem will be cured when the Print to Video instruction is given.

Selecting Print to Video is often the final stage of the editing process. Think of it as getting the release print off to the lab once the hard work in the cutting room has been done.

1 Select the File menu at the top left of Final Cut Pro and scroll down to Print to Video.

2 Release the mouse button and a box will appear giving you many options to choose from. Check those boxes which apply to your specific needs.

File	Edit	View	Mark	Mo
New				▶
New Project				⇧⌘N
Open...				⌘O
Open Recent				▶
Close Window				⌘W
Close Tab				⌃W
Close Project				
Save Project				⌘S
Save Project As...				⇧⌘S
Save All				⌥⌘S
Revert Project				
Restore Project...				
Import				▶
Export				▶
Send To				▶
Batch Export				
Batch Capture...				⌃C
Log and Capture...				⌘8
Log and Transfer...				⇧⌘8
Media Manager...				
Reconnect Media...				
Set Logging Bin				
Print to Video...				⌃M

Add color bars if you wish and enter a duration for the amount of bars you wish to record. Instruct Final Cut Pro if you want black to be recorded after the bars. Enter a title for your production in the text column and select Print Entire Media or Print In to Out depending upon your requirements. If you choose the Print In to Out option you need to mark 'in' and 'out' points in the Timeline.

3 Once you are satisfied that you have correctly selected the options you require click the OK box. The computer will pause as all the elements are gathered together.

Now sit back and enjoy your movie. It is worth keeping a close eye on the output. Print to Video is the last stage in the editing process (unless you are using it to label sections of a work in progress) and therefore it is wise to make sure everything is exactly right as the signal is recorded onto tape. Once you have at least one master safely dubbed you can relax knowing that the vital information has made it from the original camera masters, onto your computer's hard drives, through the editing process, and finally back onto digital tape. Don't forget to do a second and maybe even a third backup. This may just help you to sleep better at night.

Other Forms of Distribution

Final Cut Pro is designed as a video editor, however, just because it is designed to work with video does not mean that your final output must end up on video-tape. There are other forms of distribution in this modern world that need to be considered; for example: DVD, CD-ROM, iPod, Mobile Phone, PowerPoint and Internet delivery.

For most purposes, those on limited budgets would acquire and edit the mate-rial on DV/DVCam or HDV tape before compressing to another format. If possi-ble back up your program to tape – also compress the final edit into a single file which may be the native codec used to edit the program or another format. Backing up of material is often a neglected area of the editing room. Losing an entire program can be a hard way to learn 'always backup!'

QuickTime is a cross-platform (Mac and PC) technology designed and developed by Apple. This is often the format of choice for both Internet delivery and CD-ROM production. QuickTime is powerful and achieves results. It is particularly suited to producing encoded files on a Mac for the simple reason that QuickTime is part of the Mac operating system. It had been described as the 'the thing' that makes video on the Mac possible. However, before choosing the exact form of compression, you need information as to how and where the product will be used.

When outputting to standard definition DVD MPEG-2 is the format to be used. For high definition DVDs H.264 is the format of choice. Both formats work with QuickTime.

To output compressed files using Final Cut Pro you can choose to export using Compressor, which runs as a separate application to Final Cut Pro, or you can export Using QuickTime Conversion.

Compressor

Compressor is a program designed to encode files to different formats. It runs as a separate application to Final Cut Pro, though the two programs have been built to work together. The first release of the software was aimed primarily at DVD authoring and encoding files to MPEG-2. The capability was also there to encode files to QuickTime, AIFF and MPEG-4 for Internet delivery.

Compressor has evolved and improved. Using what Apple terms as 'optical flow technology' it is possible to produce high-quality format conversions. One can encode from NTSC to PAL and vice versa; from standard definition to high definition; images can be processed to H.264 for high definition DVD production or encoded for iPod use. The algorithms used in Compressor are the same algorithms used in Shake which is Apple's affordable high-end digital compositing application. Shake has been used to create visual effects for feature films such as Star Wars Episode 3, The Matrix and Lord of the Rings. The output quality has been described as being 'absolutely pristine.'

The brilliant thing about Compressor, aside from the output quality, is that it is very easy to use. Apple has always been the 'master of the interface' and they have lived up to that reputation with the latest version of Compressor. One can use the built-in Apple presets or one can create their own.

The following is a brief overview of how to get results using Compressor. Like many software applications, Final Cut Pro included, one can use the program on a very simple or more sophisticated level. Even using Compressor at the most basic of levels can still produce excellent results.

Let's get started.

Working with Compressor 3

Nothing gets easier than this. Using Compressor is as simple as following these steps:

1. Select a Sequence or clip to Export from Final Cut Pro.

2. Export your Clip or Sequence from Final Cut Pro into Compressor.

3. Choose a format which you wish to encode your material to.

4. Define a destination – meaning where you want your encoded files to be stored.

5. Press the Submit button to start the encoding process.

These above steps are possibly the most basic overview anyone could give to work with Compressor, however, providing you can fulfill these then you will get results.

1 Highlight a Sequence or Clip in the Browser of Final Cut Pro, or click in the Timeline to make a Sequence active.

2 Choose the File menu, top left of screen and scroll to Export Using Compressor.

The Compressor interface will now open in front of you.

3 Choose Window Layouts and the display of the interface

can then be set. Run through the options and see the different layouts. Don't be intimidated by the options. Compressor is very simple to use. At this stage there are two windows you need to concern yourself with – the Batch window and the Settings window. The Batch window is where you line up your files to be encoded and Settings is where you choose the encoding format.

Batch Window   **Settings**

There is certainly no reason why you must encode one file at a time. The Batch window is termed 'Batch' as it provides the means to encode many files.

If you choose to Export several Sequences or Clips individually from Final Cut Pro these will be represented by separate Tabs ready to encode.

If you highlight several Clips or Sequences within Final Cut Pro and then choose Export Using Compressor from the file menu these will be represented within a single Batch window with all the files in one area.

4   Go to the Settings window and click the triangle to the right of the presets to reveal the encoding options. You need to choose an option which you wish to encode to.

The settings are categorized into separate areas – you can choose to encode to Apple devices such as Apple TV or iPod; there are options to encode to DVD at various levels of quality (MPEG-2 for standard definition DVDs or H.264 for high definition DVDs); you can choose MPEG-1, MPEG-4 or H.264 for Internet delivery; there are various settings within **Formats** to encode to MPEG-1, MPEG-2, MPEG-4, and QuickTime options. Within **Other workflows** one can choose various setting from NTSC-PAL and vice versa; Settings for **Mobile Devices**, **Podcasting** and the **Web** are also offered. This is a powerful application which offers many encoding possibilities.

5 Choose an encoding option from the Settings window and drag it into the Batch window where indicated. Release your mouse button.

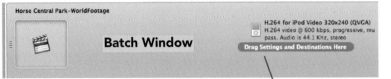

In the above example the file will be encoded for Video iPod at the frame size of 320 × 240. It really is as simple as drag and drop.

The setting you have chosen will now be displayed in the Batch window with Source indicated to the right. This means the file produced will be stored in the same area as the original file. This can be convenient some of the time but it is also useful to manually define where the encoded file will be placed.

6 Control-click the area labeled **Source** and you can then manually set the destination where the encoded file will be stored.

7 Press the Submit button at the base of the Batch window and the encoding process will begin.

8 Press the Batch Monitor icon at the top of the Batch Window and then click This Computer. You can then monitor the progress bar to get an idea of how long it will take for the encoding process to complete.

Batch Monitor

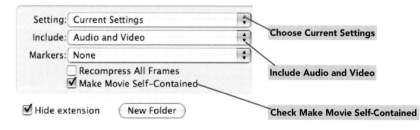

Note: if you export your files into Compressor from Final Cut Pro you will not be able to continue editing as the encoding process ties up Final Cut Pro. To get around this problem first export your Sequence/s or Clip/s from Final Cut Pro as a **Self-Contained Movie**, using **Export as QuickTime Movie** – alternatively use **Export Using QuickTime**. If you choose **Export as QuickTime Movie** make sure you check the box **Make Movie Self-Contained**. This means an entire duplicate of your film will be encoded. Once this process is complete click the

Add File icon at the top of the Compressor interface or drag the file you have created directly from its location on hard-drive and

Add File

into the Batch window of Compressor. Choose a format, begin the encoding process and then continue editing with Final Cut Pro.

Export Using QuickTime Conversion

When compressing video for the web, CD-ROM or DVD, decisions must be made about what level of compression will be used. When compressing large amounts of data there are always compromises which must be made. For example, when preparing material for Internet delivery the goal is to reduce the overall file size to a minimum while maintaining the best possible quality.

The purpose of this section is not to give detailed instructions of how to achieve these forms of output, what levels of compression to use, and exactly how to go about this – but rather to give you an overview of the areas you need to explore. There are entire books written about compression and the best ways to achieve results. What I will provide here is an introduction to the compression process using QuickTime as a means for facilitating the conversion process, and how it can be achieved using the tools provided with Final Cut Pro.

1 Highlight a Sequence or clip you wish to export in the Browser of Final Cut Pro.

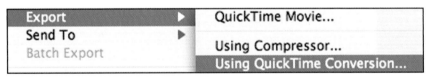

2 Choose the File menu, scroll to Export. Choose Using QuickTime Conversion.

3 Look to the bottom of the window that opens. Next to the word Format is a bar labeled QuickTime Movie. Click this bar to reveal a selection of options. You need to choose the setting appropriate to the purpose you are working towards.

Some of these options were available using Compressor, however, there are other options which are not. For example, you can export as an AVI file – used for creating files compatible with Windows Media Player or you could choose to export a single frame as a still image.

Be aware that under each of the possible compression choices are further options. For example, if you choose QuickTime Movie and click the Options setting to the right, then you can choose the quality of the video, which format you wish to compress the video to, and the audio sample rate.

You need to experiment. Look through the options, make a choice, export a movie and see the results. You can set different levels of compression, different samples rates for sound, decide whether the movie is to be prepared for Internet streaming or not. There is no easy option. You really need to know what you are trying to achieve before you start.

And, as you can see to the right, there are other possibilities to consider beyond simply choosing QuickTime.

Audio, for example, can be exported as an AIFF file. When exporting as an AIFF file consider: is the sound mono or stereo? what is the sample rate?

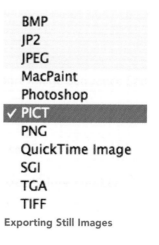

Animation
Apple Intermediate Codec
Apple Pixlet Video
Apple VC H.263
BMP
Cinepak
Component Video
DV - PAL
DV/DVCPRO - NTSC
DVCPRO - PAL
DVCPRO HD 1080i50
DVCPRO HD 1080i60
DVCPRO HD 720p60
DVCPRO50 - NTSC
DVCPRO50 - PAL
Graphics
H.261
H.263
✓ H.264
HDV 1080i50
HDV 1080i60
HDV 720p30
JPEG 2000
Motion JPEG A
Motion JPEG B
MPEG IMX 525/60 (30 Mb/s)
MPEG IMX 525/60 (40 Mb/s)
MPEG IMX 525/60 (50 Mb/s)
MPEG IMX 625/50 (30 Mb/s)
MPEG IMX 625/50 (40 Mb/s)
MPEG IMX 625/50 (50 Mb/s)
MPEG-4 Video
None
Photo - JPEG
Planar RGB
PNG
Sorenson Video
Sorenson Video 3
TGA
TIFF
Uncompressed 10-bit 4:2:2
Uncompressed 8-bit 4:2:2
Video

Recommended
8.000
11.025
12.000
16.000
22.050
24.000
32.000
44.100
✓ 48.000
64.000
88.200
96.000
192.000

Sound Settings

Format: Linear PCM

Channels: Stereo (L R)

Rate: 48.000

☐ Show Advanced Settings

Linear PCM Settings:

Sample size: 16   ⬍ bits
        ☐ Little Endian
        ☐ Floating Point
        ☐ Unsigned

(Cancel) (OK)

Exporting Audio

BMP
JP2
JPEG
MacPaint
Photoshop
✓ PICT
PNG
QuickTime Image
SGI
TGA
TIFF

Exporting Still Images

Images can be exported as Still Images. Choose PNG, TIFF, Pict or Photoshop to name just a few of the options.

If all this sounds confusing it is because we are dealing with a confusing subject – video and audio compression is constantly evolving and therefore changing. However, having access to the tools gives you access to the knowledge you need to work within this area. The beauty of working on the computer is you always get a second shot at it, and a third, fourth and hundred and thirty-first shot if you need it. A little bit of knowledge will take you a long way and your knowledge will accumulate as you go. Remember – knowledge is power! The power of distribution is at your fingertips through the process of compression. Press the buttons, wait for the encoding, and see the result.

H.264 Encoding

H.264 is a codec which was introduced with QuickTime 7 and is used for encoding files for HD DVD production, iPod, AppleTV and internet delivery of video material. H.264 can be used to produce very high quality video for distribution without creating huge files.

It is important to understand that H.264 is a distribution format and not an editing format. It's primary purpose is to get material out there so that people can play content on their computers, DVD players and other devices.

Over time expect H.264 to become more widely used as HD pushes SD content to the sidelines. H.264 is a codec that compresses well, can be used for many different purposes and can produce extremely high quality video for internet download.

Expect H.264 integration with Flash by the time you read this.

To check out the incredible quality of H.264 go to:
http://www.apple.com/quicktime/hdgallery/

ProRes 422

ProRes 422 is a new codec built into Final Cut Pro 6 designed for editing high bandwidth content such as uncompressed HD and SD files. One of the main benefits of the codec is it provides uncompressed high definition quality at standard definition data-rates. The quality difference between ProRes 422 files and uncompressed HD or SD has been described as being visually indistinguishable – even after multiple generations of re-encodes.

The strength of ProRes is that it can take large files and shrink them down into a smaller size. Because the data rates are low one can work with portable Firewire drives and get uncompressed HD quality.

ProRes is very efficient with bandwidth demands – as a result this codec provides an alternative for edit facilities which have traditionally relied on expensive RAID setups to be able to move around huge uncompressed HD files – this can now be done with ProRes files which are much more manageable and much smaller in size.

ProRes is 4:2:2 which means the format is full bandwidth. Unlike some other formats ProRes provides full 1920 × 1080 images or 1280 × 720 with different frame rates and with full chroma specification for those formats. ProRes is therefore suitable for effects production where high quality output is needed.

Animation	Animation
Apple Intermediate Codec	Apple Intermediate Codec
Apple Pixlet Video	Apple Pixlet Video
Apple ProRes 422	Apple ProRes 422
Apple ProRes 422 (HQ)	**Apple ProRes 422 (HQ)**

Notice there are two separate quality setting for ProRes: Apple ProRes 422 and AppleProRes 422 (HQ). HQ, as you might have guessed, stands for High Quality and is particularly good for producing encodes with very few compression artifacts.

While some formats are computationally difficult to edit with, such as HDV, ProRes is designed for the editing environment. It can be used to process material that requires rendering for the HDV or XDCam format, or it can be edited natively. When using ProRes in combination with HDV or XDCam this gets around some of the issues these formats suffer from due to the MPEG recording process.

ProRes has therefore been designed as an edit format, whereas H.264 is still Apple's preferred distribution format. H.264 can be used for web video, the iPod, the iPhone, Apple TV and HD DVDs.

When it comes to editing, ProRes has exceptionally high quality, low data rates and is built right into Final Cut Pro 6, ready for you to access.

Working with ProRes

To talk about working with ProRes on one level can be summed up by saying it is the same as working with any format in Final Cut Pro: you set up your Timeline, you edit, you output.

On another level it isn't really as straightforward as that.

Working in DV feels different to working in DVCPro HD; working in HDV feels different to working with 10-bit uncompressed SD. Some formats are slow to render, others zip along like a pepped up sports car; some codecs are slow to respond when dragging through the Timeline.

When working with Offline RT files in Final Cut everything is snappy, quick and fluid without a hint of hesitation. And the rendering process is joyfully quick. That's because Offline RT uses the PhotoJPG codec which compresses the signal heavily so that the footage take up very little space on hard drive. As it is compressed into small files this means it is easy for the computer to work with. The data rates are very low.

So it is with ProRes.

If you want to experience what I'm talking about then render off some DV Footage as 10 Bit Uncompressed standard definition. See how that performs in the Timeline of Final Cut Pro. Then render off some ProRes footage.

Feel the difference…

If you don't know how to do the above then follow the instructions below. Essentially rendering from one codec to another using Final Cut is the same each time. You've just got to pick the codec you want to work with.

Converting Files to ProRes

This can be achieved in three ways:

1. Export using QuickTime Movie.

2. Export using QuickTime Conversion.

3. Export Using Compressor.

File | Edit | View | Mark | Mo

New ▶
New Project ⇧⌘N
Open... ⌘O
Open Recent ▶
Close Window ⌘W
Close Tab ⌃W
Close Project

Save Project ⌘S
Save Project As... ⇧⌘S
Save All ⌥⌘S
Revert Project
Restore Project...

Import ▶
Export ▶ | **QuickTime Movie...**
Send To ▶
Batch Export | Using Compressor...
Using QuickTime Conversion...

Setting: Current Settings
Include: Audio and Video
Markers: Chapter Markers
☐ Recompress All Frames
☑ Make Movie Self-Contained

☐ Hide extension (New Folder) (Cancel)

Export to ProRes Using QuickTime Movie

1 Highlight the file you wish to convert in the Browser of Final Cut Pro.

2 Choose File and then Export Using QuickTime Movie.

3 Click where Current Settings is displayed and a drop-down menu will appear. Here you have a list of settings to choose from including different sizes and frame-rates. Choose the ProRes setting to which you wish to encode your video.

4 At the top of the window which now appears you should

name your file and choose where you wished the file to be saved. Also check that Make Movie Self-Contained is checked.

Apple ProRes 422 (HQ) 1280x720 24p 48 kHz
Apple ProRes 422 (HQ) 1280x720 25p 48 kHz
Apple ProRes 422 (HQ) 1280x720 30p 48 kHz
Apple ProRes 422 (HQ) 1280x720 60p 48 kHz
Apple ProRes 422 (HQ) 1440x1080 24p 48 kHz
Apple ProRes 422 (HQ) 1440x1080 25p 48 kHz
Apple ProRes 422 (HQ) 1440x1080 30p 48 kHz
Apple ProRes 422 (HQ) 1440x1080 50i 48 kHz
Apple ProRes 422 (HQ) 1440x1080 60i 48 kHz
Apple ProRes 422 (HQ) 1920x1080 24p 48 kHz
Apple ProRes 422 (HQ) 1920x1080 25p 48 kHz
Apple ProRes 422 (HQ) 1920x1080 30p 48 kHz
Apple ProRes 422 (HQ) 1920x1080 50i 48 kHz
Apple ProRes 422 (HQ) 1920x1080 60i 48 kHz
Apple ProRes 422 (HQ) NTSC 48 kHz
Apple ProRes 422 (HQ) PAL 48 kHz
Apple ProRes 422 1280x720 24p 48 kHz
Apple ProRes 422 1280x720 25p 48 kHz
Apple ProRes 422 1280x720 30p 48 kHz
Apple ProRes 422 1280x720 60p 48 kHz
Apple ProRes 422 1440x1080 24p 48 kHz
Apple ProRes 422 1440x1080 25p 48 kHz
Apple ProRes 422 1440x1080 30p 48 kHz
Apple ProRes 422 1440x1080 50i 48 kHz
Apple ProRes 422 1440x1080 60i 48 kHz
Apple ProRes 422 1920x1080 24p 48 kHz
Apple ProRes 422 1920x1080 25p 48 kHz
Apple ProRes 422 1920x1080 30p 48 kHz
Apple ProRes 422 1920x1080 50i 48 kHz
Apple ProRes 422 1920x1080 60i 48 kHz
Apple ProRes 422 NTSC 48 kHz
Apple ProRes 422 PAL 48 kHz

5 Press Save. (Save)

Once your file is saved you can then Import it into Final Cut Pro and then begin editing in the ProRes format. Remember to set your Easy Setup or when Final Cut Pro asks if you wish to match your Sequence to that of the clip click Yes. (Yes)

Warning – This clip does not match this sequence's settings.

For best performance your sequence and External Video should be set to the format of the clips you are editing.

Change sequence settings to match the clip settings?

(No) (Yes)

Encoding to ProRes Using QuickTime Conversion

1 Highlight the file you wish to convert in the Browser of Final Cut Pro.

2 Choose File and then Export Using QuickTime Conversion.

3 Click Options.

4 Click Settings under Video and from the drop-down list choose either Apple ProRes422 or Apple ProRes422 (HQ).

5 Click OK and save your file.

Encoding to ProRes Using Compressor

File	Edit	View	Mark	Mo
New				▶
New Project				⇧⌘N
Open...				⌘O
Open Recent				▶
Close Window				⌘W
Close Tab				^W
Close Project				
Import				▶
Export				▶
Send To				▶
Batch Export				

QuickTime Movie...
Using Compressor...
Using QuickTime Conversion...

1 Highlight the file you wish to convert in the Browser of Final Cut Pro

2 Choose File and then Export Using Compressor.

In the Settings window of the Compressor interface scroll to QuickTime which contains 5 separate settings. It is here that you will find ProRes.

3 Drag the ProRes setting onto your file in the Batch Window.

BalloonEdit-ProRes-ProRes

Apple ProRes 422 ‖ Source

Batch Window

4 Set a destination.

5 Press Submit.

Batch Monitor

6 Press Batch to monitor the status of your file as it encodes.

Settings | Destinations

9 Settings

▶ MPEG-1
1 Setting

▶ MPEG-2
3 Settings

▶ MPEG-4
1 Setting

▼ QuickTime
5 Settings

Settings

Apple Intermediate Codec (AIC)
Apple Intermediate Codec with audio AAC audio at 48kHz. Settings based off the source resolution and frame-rate.

Apple ProRes 422
AppleProRes 422 video with audio pass-through. Settings based off the source resolution and frame-rate.

H.264
QuickTime H.264 video with PCM audio at 48 kHz. Settings based off the source resolution and frame-rate.

Uncompressed 10-bit
Uncompressed 10-bit with audio pass-through. Settings based off the source resolution and frame-rate.

When to Use ProRes

As mentioned earlier one of the big advantages of ProRes is that it enables one to shrink down large files to consume a smaller amount of hard drive space with a lesser throughput of data.

Size	1.3 GB
Last Modified	Mon, May 7, 2007, 22:56
Tracks	1V, 2A
Vid Rate	25 fps
Frame Size	1024 x 576
Compressor	Uncompressed 10-bit 4:2:2
Data Rate	26.6 MB/sec
Pixel Aspect	**Uncompressed 10-Bit 4:2:2**

Look to the examples to the left for proof of just how efficient ProRes is with bandwidth.

The item properties to the left show that the file format is 10-bit uncompressed standard definition video which runs at a data rate of 26.6 MB per second and consumes 1.3 GB of space.

Size	302.0 MB
Last Modified	Today, 12:23
Tracks	1V, 2A
Vid Rate	25 fps
Frame Size	1024 x 576
Compressor	Apple ProRes 422
Data Rate	6.1 MB/sec
Pixel Aspect	**Apple ProRes 422**

When this is encoded to Apple ProRes the file size is 302 MB with a data rate of 6.1 MB per second. And when encoded to ProRes 422(HQ) the result is a file of 444 MB with a data rate of 9MB per second.

For lower bandwidth formats, which don't have vast storage and data-through-put requirements, there may be no need to use ProRes. ProRes files can sometimes end up larger than the original file, encoding from standard definition DV, for example. But for more demanding formats there are definite advantages. So ProRes does exactly what Apple says. It makes large files smaller enabling them to run at lower data rates.

So when should one use ProRes? – whenever you are using a format which gulps huge amounts of storage space and is so taxing on your processor that your sys-

Size	444.2 MB
Last Modified	Today, 12:26
Tracks	1V, 2A
Vid Rate	25 fps
Frame Size	1024 x 576
Compressor	Apple ProRes 422 (HQ)
Data Rate	9.0 MB/sec
Pixel Aspect	**Apple ProRes 422 (HQ)**

tem has to work exceptionally hard to process the data. For lower bandwidth formats, which don't have vast storage and data-through-put requirements there may be no need to use ProRes. But for other more demanding formats the advantages are clear.

Affordable High Definition

Just as DV set the world on fire when it burst on the scene in late 1995/early 1996, HDV has also captured the minds and revved up the imaginations of independent filmmakers and video professionals when it exploded like a supernova close to a decade later.

HDV has two faces. One is that of a shining goddess with incredible beauty that stands tall as being something incredible to look at. Yet in post-production stakes HDV also has the head of Medusa – look closely and you may not like what you find.

My analogies may seem somewhat over-the-top but HDV has given to us an acquisition medium which provides incredible quality at an amazing price. But when it comes to editing the images unfortunately the picture has been muddied by the difficulties which are inherent with the HDV format.

The compression used with HDV is known as long GoP MPEG-2 encoding. The signal is recorded onto DV tape and requires the same amount of disc space as DV. That's where the similarity ends. In technical terms DV is a frame-based codec – every frame stands alone – while HDV (MPEG-2) use interframe compression, this is where compression takes place according to the difference between frames. This makes HDV a very computationally difficult format to work with. As such everything works slower and the computer has to work a lot harder to achieve results.

With the powerful Macs of today, when editing HDV, everything may appear to be working as normal, particularly if it is cuts only in your HDV timeline. But start adding the layers and effects and suddenly you may find that everything becomes unwieldy.

This is because MPEG is muddy. It's all mashed together in a way where a single frame is designated as the master frame for what is known as a Group of Pictures (GOP). Each GOP occurs every 15 frames with Sony HDV or with the JVC system, HDV2 or short GOP MPEG-2, the frames are 6 frames apart. So each of the frames in the GOP, other than the master frame, is created by referring to the master frame – analysing what moves and changes in all the other frames that proceed it – and then building each of the frames in the GOP for Final Cut

Pro to access. Sounds complicated and it is. The result is a codec that is cheap and sometimes dirty, difficult for your computer to work with, but which can also produce very good pictures.

Sony HVR-Z1 HDV Camcorder: 15 frame GOP structure, records HDV2

JVC HD-100 HDV Camcorder: 6 frame GOP structure, records HDV 1

Panasonic HVX-200 DVCPro HD Camcorder: Records DVCPro HD, a frame-basaed codec, which uses 4 times the bandwidth of HDV

Working Around the HDV Problem

There are alternatives. A method I have worked with is to transcode my HDV footage to the Panasonic DVCPro HD codec. The important point to understand is that DVCPro HD, as a format, is frame independent. Every frame stands alone. This is huge at many levels. First, each frame that is recorded can be edited in and out as you choose. Also, each frame is independently capturing data and assigning compression value to important areas of the frame (like details in the shadows and color values). At no time during recording does the next frame cause the algorithm to give away detail, as it does in HDV recording.

However, converting footage to the DVCPro HD codec requires one to jump through several technical hoops and hurdles. The conversion can be done inside your Mac by using Batch Export.

Batch Export In Final Cut Pro

1 Highlight in the Browser those items which you want to Export.

2 Choose File and scroll to Batch Export.

The Export Cue will now appear showing the items you chose to export.

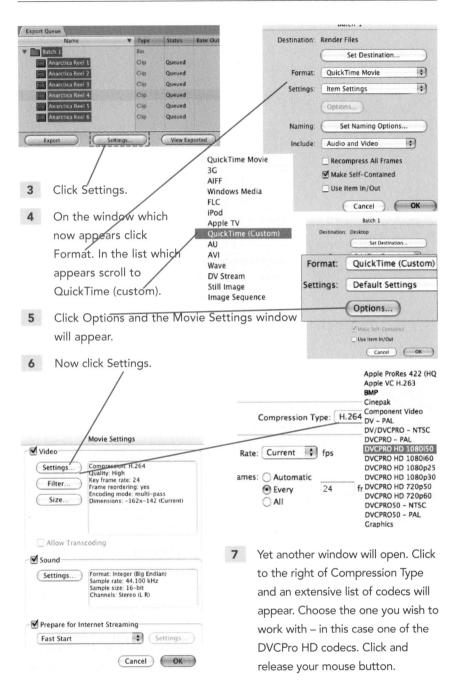

3 Click Settings.

4 On the window which now appears click Format. In the list which appears scroll to QuickTime (custom).

5 Click Options and the Movie Settings window will appear.

6 Now click Settings.

7 Yet another window will open. Click to the right of Compression Type and an extensive list of codecs will appear. Choose the one you wish to work with – in this case one of the DVCPro HD codecs. Click and release your mouse button.

8   Once you have set the Codec, back in the Movie Settings window uncheck the box where it says Prepare for Internet Streaming. Click OK.

9   Now, back at the Batch Window – check the Destination has been set. This is where your encoded files will end up on hard drive.

Once the destination is set press OK.

10 Now – back at the Export Queue window you are ready to encode. You have set the video format and destination, now press Export and all the files you have selected will be encoded to the format and location you have specified.

Wait and be patient. When you are converting to DVCPro HD it is going to take time. Don't forget you're coming from HDV which is muddy to begin with. What you are doing is sifting through the mud and cleaning it all up to work, literally, as a frame-based codec.

My experiences with editing DVCPro HD is that the format is super robust. No crashes for days on end. The downside to DVCPro HD is that it takes up 4 times the space of DV or HDV, so therefore a 500 GB drive which gives close to 37 hours of storage when working with DV or HDV will give less than 10 hours when working with the DVCPro HD codec.

The Apple Intermediate Codec (AIC)

An alternative to editing HDV is to edit with what is known as the Apple Intermediate Codec or AIC. This is a frame-based codec which, like DVCPro HD, produces large file sizes. 1080i AIC clips are four times the size of DV or HDV files.

AIC also involves a re-encode and therefore there is a barely imperceptible drop in quality from the original HDV files. This provides a quick and easy way to edit HDV files though one needs to be aware that the original timecode is lost on capture making recapture, in the event of disaster, impossible.

The procedure for setting up your system to work with the AIC codec is simple.

1 Choose Apple Intermediate Codec from the Easy Set-up at the frame rate which you are working with.

2 Got to Log and Capture.

You will notice that you do not get a Log and Capture window to work with. All you get is a very basic window which provides the means to capture your footage. There is no facility to choose audio or video independently and no means to capture timecode. This is capture on the most basic of levels. The most you get is to name your clips. Think of it like using Capture Now without being able to access the Timecode information.

3 Capture your material – one clip at a time, or one tape at a time.

One your clips are captured, set up an Apple Intermediate Codec Timeline and begin editing.

Rendering will be much slower than you are used to with DV though nothing like as slow as when working with HDV. The editing process with AIC is reliable and stable. Editing is smooth and trouble free.

Encoding Using ProRes 422

Fortunately the Final Cut Pro development team at Apple keep a close watch on what is going on and they are very much aware of the difficulties the post-production community deals with. As such a new feature has been added to Final Cut Pro 6 for those working with HDV or Sony's XDCam HD format. One can now choose to render native long GoP MPEG-2 footage using the Apple ProRes 422 format. As mentioned in the previous chapter ProRes 422 has been designed to reduce massive files such as uncompressed HD files – but there is another advantage which is it is frame-based codec.

1　Set up an HDV Timeline.

2　Click in the Timeline to make it active.

3　Click the Sequence menu and scroll to Settings.

4　Click the fourth tab – Render Control.

Sequence	Effects

Render
Render All
Render Only

Settings...

5　Click the drop-down menu for Codec and choose Apple ProRes 422.

6　Click OK.

You have now set up your HDV Timeline so that all of the rendering will now be handled by ProRes. So Final Cut Pro is effectively working between MPEG-2 editing and a frame-based high quality codec. MPEG is used for the cuts only material in the HDV Timeline – while ProRes is used for everything which needs to be rendered. The result is a smoother editing experience and while it takes time to render ProRes, more so that DV, there is none of the pain of conforming the HDV signal for those areas which require rendering – at least while you are editing. When it comes to output we find ourselves staring back at the head of Medusa and another set of problems to deal with.

Conforming HDV Video...	**One needs to wait for HDV material**
Video	**to conform the GOP. This takes**
Estimated Time: About a minute	**time. When working with HDV you**
34%	**have to both conform and render.**

Previewing Your HDV Signal As DV Over Firewire

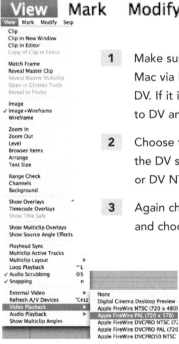

View   Mark   Modify   Sequence   Effects   Tools

1 Make sure your camera/deck is connected to your Mac via Firewire. Switch it on and set the input to DV. If it is an HDV device make sure the format is set to DV and not HDV.

2 Choose the View menu in Final Cut Pro and select the DV standard you are working with (i.e., DV-PAL or DV NTSC).

3 Again choose the View menu, scroll to External Video and choose All Frames.

Provided you have a television connected to your deck or camera you can then watch your footage in SD as you edit in HD.

Video Playback	▶	Apple FireWire NTSC (720 x 480)
Audio Playback	▶	Apple FireWire PAL (720 x 576)
Show Multiclip Angles		Apple FireWire DVCPRO NTSC (720 x 480)
		Apple FireWire DVCPRO PAL (720 x 576)

First choose Video playback and set to the DV format you wish to output and then select External Video – All Frames – the shortcut is Apple + F12.

External Video	▶	✓ Off	
Refresh A/V Devices		All Frames	⌘F12
Video Playback	▶	Single Frames	
Audio Playback	▶	Show Current	⌥F12

Previewing Your HD Signal Without Firewire

A fantastic feature of Final Cut Pro, when editing in high definition, is the ability to preview your footage as a HD signal right on your computer monitor as you work. It used to be that one needed to purchase an expensive HD monitor to watch HD footage – in today's world HD material can be viewed directly on a computer monitor.

View   Mark   Modify   Sequence   Effects   Tools

If you are working with dual monitors the process is ideal as you can have one display set to the Final Cut Pro interface and the other to preview the HD signal. If you are working with a single monitor, or a laptop without a second monitor attached, then one can flick between the Final Cut Pro interface and the HD display.

Video Playback	▶	None
Audio Playback	▶	Digital Cinema Desktop Preview – Main
Show Multiclip Angles		Digital Cinema Desktop Preview
		Digital Cinema Desktop Preview – Full Screen
		Digital Cinema Desktop Preview – Raw

Above: Dual Monitor Display choose Digital Cinema Desktop Preview

1   Choose the View menu and scroll to Video Playback.

2   Choose Digital Cinema Desktop Preview Main (for single monitor setup) or Digital Cinema Desktop Preview for a dual monitor setup.

Refresh A/V Devices	⌥F12	✓ Digital Cinema Desktop Preview – Main
Video Playback	▶	Apple FireWire NTSC (720 x 480)
Audio Playback	▶	Apple FireWire PAL (720 x 576)
Show Multiclip Angles		Apple FireWire DVCPRO NTSC (720 x 480)

Above: Single Monitor Display choose Digital Cinema Desktop Preview – Main

3 Select the View menu and scroll to All Frames (the shortcut is Apple + F12).

External Video	▶	✓ Off
Refresh A/V Devices	⌥F12	All Frames
Video Playback	▶	Single Fram
Audio Playback	▶	
Show Multiclip Angles		Show Curre

You can then preview your HD signal as you work. This system works fine for both HD and SD signals, though the real benefit is that it provides a low-cost way of viewing HD material as you edit without external hardware or investing in expensive monitors.

One needs to begin thinking differently when working with HDV and the other HD formats. The tapeless workflow already exists in the post-production environment as soon as the footage touches your hard drives, regardless of whether the rushes originated on tape or not. Capture or Transfer this material into Final Cut Pro and then, once your production is cut, decide how you wish to archive the finished edit. When working with HD, encoding files and storing the finished edit on some form of optical disc or hard drive can make more sense then going back to tape.

What Next?

We're a long way from the days when Beta SP ruled the video market. DV with its simplicity and reliability is still strong but diminishing as the HD formats becomes a priority amongst many in the video community. There are other developments at the higher levels of video production as systems which promise the quality of film emerge as strong contenders in the high-end world of feature film production. Check out http://www.red.com to find out more about what's in store for those wishing to shoot and edit video at film resolution.

And amongst all the turmoil and change, right at the epicenter of the storm Final Cut Pro stands as a mature, reliable and affordable post-production system, catering to all formats at all levels. Final Cut works the same whether it is DV or HDV or any format which is thrown at it. The interface does not change. What does change is the method, codec and settings by which the media is processed. Which buttons you press when editing, where your fingers fly as your creative mind taps away at the keyboard to produce your cuts and dissolves, sound mixes and effects, that is all format independent. This is one of the great strengths of Final Cut Pro as an editing system.

MULTICAM

Working with Multiple Cameras

There are two ways to cut between multiple camera sources. The most efficient way in terms of time is to cut live. This requires each of the cameras to be plugged into a vision switcher which is then used to mix the program in real time.

The output of the vision mixer is then recorded to tape or broadcast live.

The other way is do it in post. This used to be a nightmare. It was immensely time consuming and difficult to achieve. With Final Cut Pro and Multicam this is dream-way of working.

For over a decade I punched buttons on vision switchers in live studio environments. I directed live programs and earned my living as a studio director. As such, the way I use Final Pro with Multicam is very similar to using a live vision switcher. I more or less cut the program live and fine tune the results either as I work, or after the live cut has been done.

The key to using Multicam in Final Cut Pro begins with acquisition. When shooting, make sure that all cameras run continuous. No switching off, no stop-starting, continuous shooting is critical.

If this rule is adhered to, it will make your time in post-production very simple indeed.

Mixing Live vs. Cutting in Post

Before non-linear systems were around, online edit suites with many tape machines running in sync were used to simulate a live multi-camera environment. Threaded up on each of the tape machines were the individual reels or each of the cameras takes. The machines were then run in sync and each source would be cut on a vision switcher. The fact that one was working in an edit suite provided the flexibility of stop-starting or running continuous. This was the only way to do a multicam edit outside of a live studio environment.

So the advantage of doing a multi-camera edit in post is clear. In this environment one can stop-start. When doing it live you only have one shot at it. No matter how good one is as a live director/switcher the fact-of-the-matter is one can achieve better results cutting in post than in a live environment.

Preparation

Just to hammer-home the point, the success of a multi-camera shoot begins in the acquisition stage. Let all cameras roll continuous. No stop-starting.

If you shoot for an hour performance on three cameras you will end up with 3 hours of footage. If you shoot for an hour on four separate cameras you will acquire 4 hours of footage.

Once the footage has been shot for your Multicam production each of the camera angles needs to be captured into Final Cut. I strongly suggest numbering your reels on capture and labelling the captured material as Camera 1, Camera 2, Camera 3 and so-forth.

1   Open the Log and Capture window (the shortcut is Apple+8).

2   Label the Reel Number and enter a name for the clip which is to be captured.

Label the Reel Number and Description

227

3 Mark the 'in' and 'out' points for the reel.

4 Press Log Clip.

5 Capture the reel.

Now repeat the above procedure for the remaining camera angles so that you end up with the amount of reels captured that corresponds to the amount of camera angles which were filmed.

Creating Multiclips (Syncing Up the Reels)

Once your material is captured you need to make what is known as a Multiclip. A Multiclip is several clips grouped together into a single clip. This single clip references to all the camera angles which you have grouped together. Simply put, several reels are synced together and this clip, termed the Multiclip, is what you work with when cutting your Multicam sequence.

Making a Multiclip is a very easy procedure. The most involved part of the process is to sync up the different camera angles on each of the reels.

There are three ways to do this:

1 by 'In' Point

2 by 'Out' Point

3 by 'Timecode'.

Synchronize using: **In Points**
Out Points
Timecode
Aux Timecode 1
And Aux Timecode 2

The first two methods are easy to use and the way I tend to work. In fact more often than not I will sync by 'in' point.

The third method, by 'timecode', is designed to be used on jobs where matching timecode exists on each of the camera tapes. This is achieved by using a process known as jam-syncing. Unless you are working with a reliable method of jam-syncing cameras I suggest you stand clear of this method.

Syncing by 'In' Point

This is the easiest way to sync up your reels.

1   Place a clip of one of the camera angles in the Timeline.

2   Find an easy sync point to work with. If a clapperboard or handclap has been used on location then use this, otherwise an audio cue such as the first spoken word of sentence can be used. (It is useful to turn on Audio Scrubbing found under the View menu).

3   Mark an 'in' point in the Timeline.

Note: a visual and audio cue provides the ideal way to sync up separate reels. Cue to the exact point where the handclap occurs and mark an 'in' point. Do the same on each of the different reels. If no handclap or clapperboard has been used you need to find a common audio point on each of the reels.

229

4   Mark an 'out' point, if you wish to define the end point for a particular camera angle. It is not absolutely necessary to mark an 'out' point.

Repeat the above procedure with the other camera angles.

To be clear about how to sync by 'in' point you need to find a point on the tape which can be used to sync up each of the reels. An audio cue is usually a good option to work with. The best option is a combination of audio and visual cue.

If, for example, the first word of a sentence is WELCOME, then scrub frame by frame to the first utterance of the letter W. Watch the lips on the subject if these are visible, though it is possible to work with an audio cue only. So long as you can hear the audio cue, syncing up the reels can be achieved. Without an audio cue it is much more difficult.

So once a sync reference point has been established you mark the 'in' point and then repeat the procedure for each of the reels which will make up the Multiclip.

Once you have marked the 'in' point (and 'out' points if you wish to define an exit point) you need to lock these clips together through the Make Multiclip command.

1   Make sure the 'in' points are marked on each of the separate reels.

2   Highlight each of the camera angles in the Browser.

3   Select the Modify Menu and scroll down to **Make Multiclip**.

4   Sync up the reels (see page 200). Click OK.

The Multiclip will now appear in the Browser.

Working with Multiclips

If you double click the Multiclip it will open in the Viewer just like any other clip, the major difference being obvious as soon as the Multiclip is open.

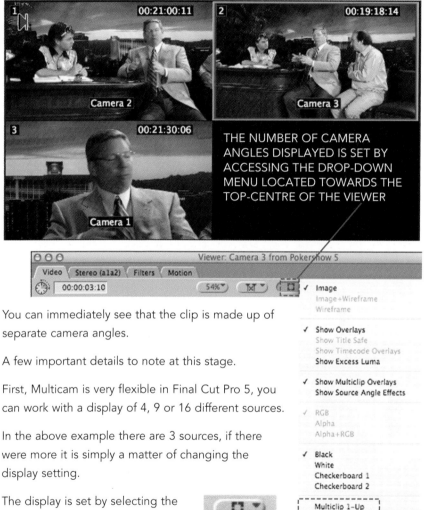

You can immediately see that the clip is made up of separate camera angles.

A few important details to note at this stage.

First, Multicam is very flexible in Final Cut Pro 5, you can work with a display of 4, 9 or 16 different sources.

In the above example there are 3 sources, if there were more it is simply a matter of changing the display setting.

The display is set by selecting the controls found under the drop-down menu toward the top center of the Viewer.

Begin by working with the 4 camera display.

Also, note that within each of the camera angle displays, there is information such as clip name and Timecode. This is useful. Providing one has labeled each reel appropriately then the display makes it easy to see which camera angle is being shown. Furthermore, you can accurately go back to any point on any of the reels by using the information provided in the timecode display.

If you hold down the Apple key you can easily slide each of the angles around within the Viewer. Therefore, you can line up the camera angles in whatever order you wish.

TO ARRANGE THE DIFFERENT CAMERA ANGLES WITHIN THE VIEWER HOLD THE APPLE KEY AND DRAG.

Before you get started with Multicam be aware that Multiclips need to be rendered. That doesn't mean you have to render everything just to see what's going on – it means a final render at the end. While you are working it all happens in real time. All video streams will play together and the live switching happens in real-time. If you find you need greater performance buy a modern Mac or boost your ram.

Cutting your Multicam Sequence

It is important to understand the relationship between the Timeline/Canvas and the Viewer when working with Multicam.

The Viewer must be set so that while you run your Multiclip in the Timeline the various camera angles play back, all running in sync, within the Viewer window.

The procedure is easy to set up.

Safe RT
✓ Unlimited RT

Play Base Layer Only

✓ Scrub High Quality

Playback Video Quality
✓ Dynamic
High
Medium
Low

Playback Frame Rate
✓ Dynamic
Full
Half
Quarter

✓ Multiclip Playback

1   Choose the RT drop-down menu located top left of the Timeline. Scroll down and make sure that Multiclip Playback is checked. **This is vital**.

2   Edit the Multiclip you have created into the Timeline – this can be achieved by dragging the Multiclip from the Browser into the Timeline or by opening the Multiclip in the Viewer and then performing an Insert or Overwrite edit.

3   Once the Multiclip is in the Timeline double click it. The Multiclip will now open in the Viewer.

4 Click the drop-down box located at the top of the Viewer that looks like the letter X surrounded by two lines. Scroll down and select **Open.** This is important. If you do not select this, the live Multicam play-back will not work.

5 Click the yellow Scrubber Bar in the Timeline and place this at the beginning of your Multiclip sequence.

6 Press the Space Bar to play.

Providing you have followed the above steps, the Multiple angles displayed in the Viewer will play in sync while the Canvas will display the Active Angle.

7 To cut between camera angles simply click in the Viewer on each of the angles as they play in sync. The result will then appear in the Canvas.

Notice cut points in the form of blue markers appear as you switch from angle to angle. When you stop playback the cut points become cuts in the Timeline.

At any time you can stop playback and review the edits you have made. You can continue editing by simply positioning the yellow Scrubber Bar in the Timeline and pressing play. You can then continue cutting live in the Viewer.

If you find that playback in the Viewer does not follow that in the Timeline then repeat points 3 to 5 listed on the previous pages. This will make the Multiclip active and run the angles in sync in the viewer.

If the camera angles play, however they are out of sync with each other, then you need to remark the 'in' points on each of the separate reels and make a new Multiclip. The problem will be that the points have not been marked correctly.

Working with Multicam without Cutting the Soundtrack

You will notice that when you cut between the various camera angles that picture and sound cut together. This is far from ideal, due to the fact that most often with a multicamera shoot a master camera is used to record sound. For example, a concert will have a line-feed out from the mixing deck plugged into one of the cameras. Thus the last thing one would want is to cut between line sound and that recorded through the camera mics.

My method is to take the master camera sound and lay this onto separate audio tracks in the Timeline. For example I would put the Multiclip Video onto V1 and the Multiclip Audio A1 and A2.

I would then edit the sound from the master camera onto A3 and A4.

Finally, turn off the monitoring on A1 and A2.

The result is you hear the sound from the master camera and do not hear the distracting sound of cutting between the different camera angles.

Turn off Monitoring for the Multiclip on A1 & A2

Here's an overview of the procedure to work with a Multiclip and listen to a master audio track while editing:

1 Edit the Multiclip into the Timeline – video to V1, audio to A1 and A2.

2 Edit the master soundtrack to audio tracks A3 and A4. Do not edit video – sound only!

3 Turn off the monitoring to audio tracks A1 and A2.

4 Double click your Multicam sequence to make it active in the Viewer.

5 Click the drop-down box located towards the middle of the Viewer and select Open.

6 Click the yellow Scrubber Bar in the Timeline and run your Multicam sequence. The Soundtrack you hear will be the master soundtrack playing back on A3 and A4. The sound from A1 and A2 will be mute.

The result is you hear the sound from the master camera and will not hear the distracting sound of cutting between the different camera angles.

Fine Tuning your Multicam Sequence

The beauty and power of cutting a multi-camera sequence in a post-production environment is you can get the editing just right. Better than a live cut!

There are two strategies to achieving this. First you can fine tune as you go; stop-starting and making whatever alterations are necessary.

Alternatively, you can do the entire Multicam edit as a live mix and then go back afterwards for the fine tuning.

For fine-tuning edits your best friend is the Roll tool, accessed by pressing the letter R on the keyboard or by selecting from the Toolbar. The Roll Tool looking like a figure 8 and lets you extend or reduce edits without affecting the length of your sequence. All that is affected is the duration of the shot you are extending or reducing and the shot immediately next to that which you are altering.

Once you have performed your multi-camera edit select the Roll tool and place this at the junction of a cut, then click and drag and very easily you can move the edit in either direction, lengthening or shortening the camera angles on either side.

Use the Roll Tool to extend edit to the left or right without affecting the overall duration of the Timeline.

Original edit

The edit is rolled to the left

The result is shot to the left is made shorter, while that to the right is made longer

The edit is now rolled to the right

The result is the shot to the left is made longer while that to the right is shorter

Note: as you work with the Roll Tool a display in seconds and frames will show you the change in duration to the edit you are changing.

Open 'Camera 1 [3]-Multiclip 3'
Duration (00:00:21:11)...
Make Independent Clip
Item Properties ▶
Send To ▶

Cut
Copy
Paste
Paste Attributes...
Remove Attributes...
Ripple Delete

✓ Clip Enable
Speed...
Composite Mode ▶
Dupe Frames ▶

Collapse Multiclip(s)
Active Angle [3] ▶
       [1]: Camera 2
       [2]: Camera 3
Reconnect Media...   ✓ [3]: Camera 1
Media Manager...
Capture...

Segment 1
Segment 2
Segment 3
Segment 4
Segment 5
Segment 6
Segment 7
Segment 8
Segment 9
Segment 10
Segment 11
Segment 12
Segment 13

You can also change the active angle of any part of the Multiclip, after you have cut done your 'live cut', to any other angle. Simply, Control click on any portion of the Multiclip and select the angle you wish to use. This will only affect the portion of the Multiclip on which you have Control-clicked.

Another way to change the Active Angle or a particular section of the Multiclip is to double click the Multiclip and then simply select the angle of choice. This will work whether you are playing the camera angles live or if it is stationary.

Click the angle you wish to make active and then you will have it.

If, at any point, you just can't get your Multiclip to play in the Timeline with all the angles following in the Viewer simultaneously, simply double click the Multiclip in the Timeline, select the Open command in the Viewer and then click the yellow Scrubber Bar in the Timeline. Then, press the Space Bar to play. This will get you back on track.

A repeat of the above: when the separate camera angles in the Viewer do not all play together, in sync with the Multiclip playing in the Timeline, then do the following:

1 Double click the Multiclip in the Timeline.

2 Select Open from the drop-down menu toward the center of the Viewer.

3 Click the yellow Scrubber Bar in the Timeline and position at the point you want the Multiclip to play.

4 Press the Space Bar to play.

What you are doing is making the Timeline active and instructing the Viewer to play the separate angles that make up the Multiclip in sync with that in Timeline. Play is the GO button. Everything will play together.

Always remember, as long as the camera angles are running in sync within the Viewer window, and your Multiclip is playing in the Timeline, then everything is working as it should. If any of the camera angles are out of sync with each other this is the result of incorrect syncing of clips when the 'in' or 'out' point were marked. Multiclips do not drift or ever lose sync. Everything is locked together. If anything is out of sync it is caused by incorrect sync points when the Multiclip was created.

When editing with Multicam, providing you have a camera or deck with a monitor connected to your Mac, you can then preview the out through Firewire (assuming you are working with a DV set-up). Just the same as previewing DV over Firewire – connect up your deck or camera and then plug this into a television or broadcast monitor and start cutting.

Multicam will work with DV, SD or HD. This is not a format specific feature. It works with everything.

Note: playback of HDV over Firewire can only be output as SD.

Final Tips

Multiclips can be collapsed by Control clicking and selecting the Collapse Multiclip command. This gives you the ability to make the selected active angle represent a single clip in the Timeline. Once the Multiclip is collapsed it will act like any other clip. Double click it and it will open in the Viewer. You can then place filters or any adjustments to it in the same way as any other clips.

Once collapsed multiclips or sections of multiclips can be uncollapsed by Control clicking and selecting Uncollapse Multiclip.

ϽμΕΕυ...

Composite Mode ▶

Dupe Frames ▶

Uncollapse Multiclip(s)

Note: multiple cuts within a Multiclip can be collapsed or uncollapsed by highlighting multiple sections within the Multiclip itself and then selecting either the Collapse Multiclip(s) command or the Uncollapse Multiclip(s) command. This is a quick way to deal with large sections of the Timeline in one go.

Uncollapsed Multiclip in Viewer

Collapsed Multiclip in Viewer

Dealing with 'Buttoning On and Off'

Trigger happy videographers have a tendency to hit the record button repeatedly through a filming session. By habit or instinct these people have an in-built resistance to the idea of running tape continuously in the camera. As such, you will need to know how to deal with a situation where multiple cameras have been used and there is not continuous take. Rather you may have a selection of incomplete takes, perhaps timecode breaks and switching on and off between cameras at different points.

These situations can present a nightmare situation for an editor to work with. However, none of these predicaments are a nightmare with no way out.

The solution is to make up many Multiclips and extract the good from the bad when it comes to dealing with the masses of camera rushes.

Here's the way forward:

1 Capture all of the footage.

2 Once captured, run all of the footage through DV Start/Stop Detect (found under the Mark Menu).

3 Once your footage has been processed by the DV Start/Stop Detect facility, click the triangle next to the clip to reveal a list showing every time the camera operator has hit the record button ('buttoned' on or off). If you are dealing with 4 to 10 times or less, no problem. If you are dealing with 50 or a 100 separate times then you have your work cut out for you. Never-the-less it can be done.

4 Watch through your material and identify corresponding angles which exist on the separate tapes and where the stop-starts take place. For example, you may have two cameras: one has the first 5 minutes of a performance and the other has the first 8 minutes. You can then sync up the first 5 minutes as a two camera shoot. The first camera 'buttoned' on again 10 minutes into the performance and then cut at 23 minutes. The other camera filmed continuous. So then you have ingredients needed to make another Multiclip.

It is simply a matter of marking an 'in' point; marking an 'out' point (if you wish) and then highlighting the clips and invoking the Make Multiclip command.

If there is no hand clap, slate or clapperboard to work with then finding a common audio sync point is the simplest way forward.

Syncing without Sound

The DV and HDV cameras of today are much more sophisticated than the first generation of DV cameras which appeared in 1996.

Very few early DV cameras had XLR inputs; you couldn't set the Timecode; no fold-out screens; sloppy zooms; slow response when hitting the record button; these machines were battery-eaters. Things have come a long way.

With sophistication comes complexity. As the DV cameras evolved many new features were added. To get at these features requires one to work through many menus. Some of these cameras are so menu-laden one virtually needs to be a computer programmer to get at the manual controls which are buried away like unreachable treasures.

I've seen cameramen swear at menu setups when all they want to do is switch over from camera mic to external mic. The one plugged into the XLR. The one with the good sound.

So screw-ups happen.

Perhaps the worst case scenario is no sound at all. When putting together a Multicam sequence, the key to success is getting your Multiclip right. If you get everything synced up correctly the battle is won. This is a lot harder to do if you've got no sound to work with.

In this situation the only way to sort out the problem is by use of a visual cue. You need to find a reference point where something happens. This could be easy or incredibly difficult.

If you were filming a rocket taking off with eight different cameras it would not be a difficult process. Simply line up each take of the rocket blasting off and mark an 'in' point using a common visual cue. For example, the ignition of the engines.

Yet, if you were cutting an interview with two or three separate cameras, without sound on one or more of the cameras, then this is quite difficult. Unless you are a lip reader then finding a sync point is not easy. You need to look for the subtle details: the raise of a hand, bursting into laughter, a smile, a blink of the eyes . . . these are the only reference points you will have to work with other than actually reading the lips of the person speaking.

From experience, I can tell you that these are real situations which must be dealt with in the real world of multi-camera production.

I consider Multicam in Final Cut Pro to be the launch-point for a new way of making films. In previous decades shooting with multiple cameras was shunned by small or no budget filmmakers for the simple reason that it created a nightmare in the editing and cost a fortune to hire the cameras.

The cameras are now affordable and Multicam in Final Cut Pro provides an excellent means to achieving a truly professional multi-camera edit. You can cut between 2 and 16 camera angles at any one time with everything running in sync.

Multicam works and it works well.

Having this facility integrated into Final Cut Pro makes this application a dream system that puts other, more expensive editors, to shame.

The golden age of filmmaking burns bright.

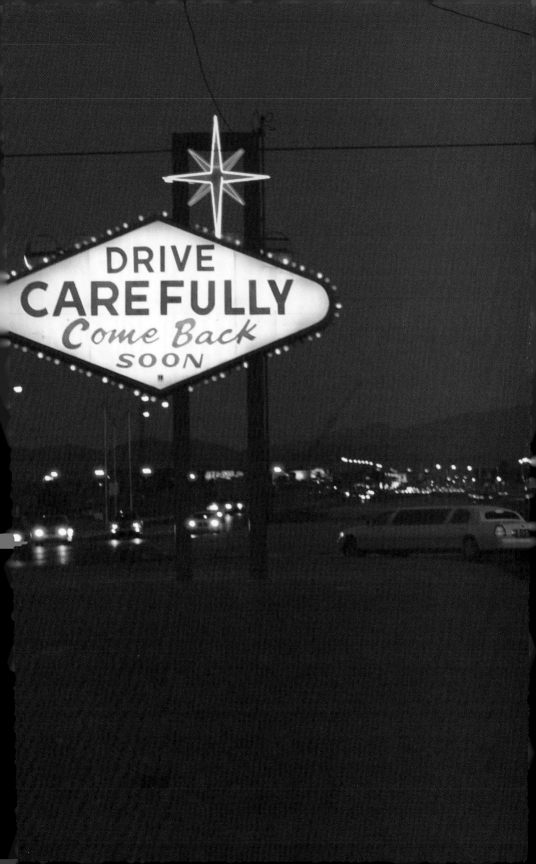

Epilog

Apple have always been individual in the way they do things. The way their machines operate, the way they look, even their screens are unique. No matter how hard the competition tries, Apple has remained a formidable force in the creative industries of the world.

The reason why Apple continues to be a success is the result of an extremely loyal customer base who refuse to abandon their platform of choice. People do not remain loyal to Apple out of some kind of blind devotion – they remain loyal because Apple machines and software serve them better than their competitors.

People like using Apple computers.

People love using Apple computers.

When it comes to Final Cut Pro, the same applies.

In a few short years Apple have created an editing system which shines bright across the murky waters of the post-production scene.

Final Cut Pro is reliable and stable. It works very well. And it works with every known format on the planet: video and film.

It is the success it is for very clear reasons:

It's easy to use.

It's powerful.

It's affordable.

A friend said to me years ago: 'You know, I don't know why Apple computer's still exist.'

They exist because the people want them to exist.

That's it.

The Future

Tape is going to go away.

A lot more is going to be done in ram.

We'll all be able to access high speed internet
from anywhere on the planet with a device no
bigger than a credit card.

And the world will keep on turning to the
beat of the silicon chip.

Apple's suite of tools will be everywhere.
In schools and offices, peoples homes
and production facilities for all types of media.

Sure there will be competing products;
high end; low end; PC and everything in between.

But for those who want the best without spending
fifty or a hundred thousand dollars, pounds or Euros,
then it's Apple technology and Mac software every step
of the way.

Because we can afford it, because it works, and because, for
the money, it's streets ahead of anything else out there.

Index